Digital
Photography
Step-by-Step

Digital
Photography
Step-by-Step

Jerry Glenwright

Collins

First published in 2002
This revised and updated edition published in 2008 by
Collins, an imprint of
HarperCollins Publishers
77–85 Fulham Palace Road
Hammersmith
London W6 8JB

The Collins website address is www.collins.co.uk

Collins is a registered trademark of HarperCollins Publishers Ltd.

12   11   10   09   08
7   6   5   4   3   2   1

This book was conceived, designed and produced by
The Ilex Press Limited
Cambridge CB2 4LX, England

Publisher: Alastair Campbell
Creative Director: Peter Bridgewater
Editorial Director: Tom Mugridge
Editor: Chris Gatcum
Art Director: Julie Weir
Design Assistant: Emily Harbison
Designer: Hugh Schermuly

A catalogue record for this book is available
from the British Library

ISBN 978 0 00 782257 7

Printed and bound in China

An Introduction to Digital

1

An Introduction to Digital...

Digital photography is the remarkable realisation of a 150-year wish-list of photographers. It offers instant gratification allied with complete mastery over the results, combined with an affordable and portable technology in an easy-to-use package. And yet digital photography is, simply, photography, just like the Daguerreotypes of yesteryear and the medium-format photos of today. Whether you take a picture using light-sensitive paper in a camera fashioned from a pinhole in a shoe box, or hold in your palm the latest hi-tech digital wonder, the end result is the same: a picture that hopefully will strike an emotional note. The difference is that with digital photography you can do what once required expensive equipment and complete darkness: manipulate images however you want...

CLICKING THE LIGHT FANTASTIC!

A photograph – conventional or digital – is a fleeting moment captured for ever. In 1839, on viewing a demonstration of the process of picture-taking, the astronomer Sir John Herschel described it as 'a miracle!' And that power to amaze, inspire, and excite continues to strike a chord even today.

The 19th century was a time of great invention. In Britain and America scientists, civil and marine engineers, architects, and experimenters in every field were developing technology for ever bigger buildings, bridges, ships, and locomotives, while surgeons too were making incredible advances in medicine. It was a time of upheaval and change, though with the emphasis firmly on the industrial rather than the cultural.

In the midst of these great endeavours, in 1826, French inventor Joseph Nicéphore Niépce attempted to find a practical use for the recent discoveries made with light-sensitive chemicals known as silver halide compounds. By marrying the artists' tool and the fairground novelty *camera obscura* (see panel) with a small square of pewter coated with silver halides suspended in a solution of asphalt, Niepce succeeded in taking the world's first photograph; an eight-hour exposure of a farmyard.

Photographs from Niepce's camera required extremely lengthy exposure times, during which the asphalt hardened and the image was captured. For this reason the process was essentially useless for all but inanimate subjects. What's more, the images were

A SHOT IN THE DARK

A phenomenon known to the ancient Greeks, the *camera obscura* (from the Latin for 'dark room') projects an outdoor scene by admitting light through a hole and recreating the scene on an opposite wall, or on a table. Unlike the camera as we know it, no means existed for recording the projected image, although artists once used small *camera obscuras* to copy from life by sketching over the projection as an aid to accurate reproduction.

dim and fuzzy. But for all their faults they were recognisable and available for others to view. They were photographs.

After some years' experimentation, Niepce met up with fellow Parisian, Louis Jacques Mandé Daguerre, who hit upon the idea of 'developing' the photo after it had been exposed rather than as a part of the exposure itself. Developing an image in this way shortened exposure times significantly. Daguerre also discovered that images could be fixed by immersing the developed photograph in a salt solution. In 1839 (several years after Niepce's death), Daguerre announced to the world the first practical photographic process. The pictures from this process, known as 'Daguerreotypes,' became extremely popular, as did the little tin photos they produced.

Daguerre's photos were 'one-shot' positive pictures. That is, the captured image was developed as a positive image (the equivalent of a print in a package of photographs) without a negative step in the process. While this might at first appear to be a perfectly reasonable approach, the only way to make a second photograph of the same image was to take an identical picture again!

Early Negatives

Briton William Henry Fox Talbot solved the problem. In 1840, Fox Talbot announced his 'Calotype' process. This added a negative stage to picture-taking (an image in which the light areas are dark and the dark areas light). Talbot's Calotype negatives could be used to make an unlimited number of positive prints on specially prepared, chemically treated paper.

One disadvantage of Talbot's paper negatives was that the imperfections in the paper produced correspondingly fuzzy images. A cousin of Niepce's, however, had the solution. Abel Niepce de Saint-Victor coated glass plates with light-sensitive chemicals embedded in the albumen of eggs. The glass negatives produced very fine pictures, but exposure times remained comparatively slow. Building on Saint-Victor's work, Frederick Scott Archer refined the chemicals in the coating and devised an improved processing method ('Collodion'),

Small and fuzzy maybe, but Daguerreotypes *(above)*, the little tin pictures created using the process devised by Louis Daguerre, were the first commercially available permanent images captured from life. The Kodak 'Box Brownie' *(left)* was the world's first camera for everyone. Containing enough film for 100 exposures, the camera was simply returned complete for processing. Suddenly, photography was a hobby almost everyone could pursue.

which reduced exposure times to two or three seconds and substantially reduced the cost to about a shilling (5 pence) for each print.

Pictures on a Plate

One final difficulty remained. Managing glass negatives was a 'wet process,' that is the plates had to be coated, exposed, and processed while wet. This cumbersome process led Dr Richard Maddox to experiment with gelatin coatings, and by 1871, Maddox had perfected a 'dry-plate' process. And when, in 1884, US bank clerk George Eastman combined lengths of the recently invented celluloid with gelatin-based photographic coatings, modern film and modern photography were born.

Amazing though photography was, the invention met with hoots of derision from artists and critics, who dismissed the process as one that was largely mechanical with little creative input. It was worthless, they said, or at best easily mastered. The truth, of course, just as much then as it is now, is that the mechanics of photography are

indeed mastered relatively easily, but the eye of the photographer is as potent a conduit for artistic expression as any painter's brush.

While the cultural elite remained sceptical, the public took photography to their hearts. Early equipment was cumbersome and the chemical processes complex and delicate, but photography could be learned by anyone who set their mind to the task.

Single-lens reflex (SLR) cameras such as this high-quality Nikon use a folding mirror to project the image from the lens to a viewfinder. This arrangement enables the photographer to see exactly what the camera sees, thereby sidestepping the possibility for parallax error.

Digital

Conventional film

When shown greatly enlarged, the visible pixelation of a good-quality digital image is comparable with the grain of conventional film.

Pocket-sized Miracle

...ame George Eastman dreamed up the
...n of a camera that could be held in the
... and carried everywhere, and which
... a roll of film. The camera would then
...mply handed over for processing at
...nted agents, such as pharmacies, and
...ned with the photographs and ready-
...d with fresh film. Eastman's invention
...went further refinement when Oskar
...ck, head of design and development
...mera manufacturer Leitz of Wetzlar,
...any, combined 35mm cine film with a
...lly designed, pocket-sized camera that
... could be taken anywhere.

Digital Leap

... more than a decade after Barnack
...oped the pocket-sized 35mm camera,
...Von Neuman in the US and Alan Turing
...itain were busy laying the foundations
...odern computer science. By the 1950s,
...uters were room-sized monsters, but the
...ines established the principles of binary
...outing. The arrival of transistors, solid
... electronics, and, eventually silicon and
...aturisation, finally paved the way for
...'s pocket-sized digital devices.

...he first digital cameras began to appear
...e end of the 1980s, along with crude
...e scanners and low-resolution laser
...ers. Resolution was abysmal, memory
...eful, and prices astronomical. But

POWER VISION

The first electronic computers filled rooms, consumed
megawatts of electricity, sported just a few dozen bits of
memory and had a 'brain' capacity that an intelligent food
processor would put to shame. By comparison, your digital
camera has a memory measured in megabytes and processing
power beyond the wildest dreams of the early computer
scientists, and all contained within a case you
can keep in a shirt pocket!

became available that offered reasonable
resolutions at sensible prices.

Today, you can buy a multimegapixel digital
camera for little more than a day's salary. Most
will provide photorealistic images in a package
that will slip easily into the pocket. You
can manipulate those images on a personal
computer, print them, and enjoy near-
professional results with remarkable ease.

Compact digital cameras
like this smart little Canon
Digital IXUS make picture-
taking easy. The camera
calculates the exposure,
automatically focuses the lens,
and captures a high-resolution
image when you fire the
shutter. All you have to do is
point it at a suitable subject!

Hardware
Made Easy

Pixels, CCDs, firmware, digital this, digital that, resolution, and connectivity... and all you wanted to do was take a picture! The camera has, without a doubt, moved firmly into the 21st century. But understanding the technology and making use of that new-found knowledge of hardware and software to get the best from your digital camera and produce fantastic photographs seems elusive. If knowledge is power, then understanding your camera is the most powerful way to perfect its use and produce images that will not only please you, but all who see them...

BITS AND PCS

'Digital camera' – the name is at once fascinating and a little frightening. It conjures up daunting lists of associated jargon. So exactly what is 'digital' and what effect does it have on picture-taking?

The word 'digital' has been in common usage for 30 years and is used to describe everything from watches and calculators to, more recently, radios, televisions, and cameras - but few understand what the term really means. While understanding the technology isn't a prerequisite for using a digital camera, some knowledge *will* enable you to maximise the opportunities the hardware offers. And, what's more, it isn't that complex.

The Future is On or Off

Turn to the dictionary for a definition of digital and you'll be rewarded with the stark description 'of digits'; not terribly helpful, but nevertheless that's the nub of what we're trying to understand. Digital technology relies on acquiring and manipulating picture, audio, or other information as a sequence of binary digits - the numbers 1 and 0 - where 1 represents the presence of data, and zero its absence. The beauty of these 1s and 0s is that they can be represented by anything which has two states (hence binary), on and off: a switch, a light bulb, or a transistor (which is, after all simply a switch) on an integrated circuit (IC).

Let's apply the binary concept of 'ons' and 'offs' to musical recording. A traditional vinyl-based recording is captured within, and

CAPTIVE IMAGES AND RESOLUTION

A digital camera works much like a conventional model, in that light passes through a lens and is recorded inside. However, in place of film, the digital camera has at its heart a chip known as a CCD (charge-coupled device). This, essentially, is a matrix of tiny light-sensitive cells. The tinier and greater the number of cells, the better the resulting image - the higher its 'resolution'. The CCD passes varying electrical charges to a device called an analogue-to-digital converter. These are transformed into 1s and 0s (binary data), and from there sent to a memory device for storage. The CCD and its cells are similar to conventional film and its silver-halide grains, in that each captures the light that makes up the resulting picture. But unlike a conventional camera, you can't change a digital camera's CCD as you can a conventional camera's film.

recreated from, a continuous groove in the vinyl, which, when fed through a transducer (a device for converting one kind of energy into another, in this case the movement of the needle into an electrical signal), produces a continuous, varying signal - one which has peaks and troughs. There is no 'on' and 'off' state, except where the music itself begins and ends. This is a called an analogue signal.

By contrast, a CD recording has no such grooves. Instead, the music is 'sampled' (examined) by a device, usually a computer, during which it is broken into a stream of tiny chunks of ons and offs, 1s and 0s. Just how tiny is vitally important, as we'll discover later on, but suffice to say that early CD recordings did not break the data into small enough bits ('binary digits'), so the quality was, for a short time, inferior in some ways to vinyl.

The Orchestra Pits

Quality issues aside, the stream of 1s and 0s is recorded as microscopic pits 'burned' onto the surface of the CD. To recreate the music, a laser scans the pits, noting where the 1s and 0s ('pit' or 'no pit') fall. After a certain amount of interpreting by clever computer programming, the CD player recreates the music. Although the sound from the CD player starts out as a sequence of ons and offs, the listener hears continuous music.

Digital Pictures

Similarly, light and shade entering a camera is divided into a stream of 1s and 0s which, when manipulated by software, reproduce the original image. Enlarge the image sufficiently and you'll see that it is in fact a series of blocks ('pixels' - more of which later), but the overall image is generally of sufficient quality to fool the eye.

Pixel

When light enters a digital camera, it is directed into a matrix of sensors that generates a variable electric charge. This charge is transformed into a binary data stream. Enlarge a digital image and eventually you'll see the tiny blocks of picture data which fool the eye into seeing a continuous image.

BUILDING BLOCKS

Resolution, pixelation, and interpolation – although they sound complicated, they are the stuff of which digital images are made. Understanding what they are will assist you in buying and using a digital camera.

On the previous pages, you were introduced to the basic concept of resolution. A simple equation describes what's required: tinier samples (and therefore more of them) equal higher-quality audio, pictures, or whatever it is that's being sampled. This is called a high sampling rate. But why should more equal better? Think of it this way. Draw a circle with a pencil around the base of a tumbler. There are two ways to find the length of the circle's circumference. The precise mathematical formula πxD (3.14 times the diameter) will provide the figure, or you can use a ruler and try to measure bits of the circumference. It follows that the tinier the bits of circumference you measure, the more accurate will be the final measurement. Big bits give a loose approximation, while smaller bits give a closer one.

Digital Approximation

So it is with pictures, sounds, and anything else that's digitised (rendered into bits of data). Greater resolution results in a digital sample that is more convincing to the eye or ear. However, it is a paradox of the digital world that whereas accuracy to the last bit is essential for correct operation (for example, a single bit of bad data can bring even a

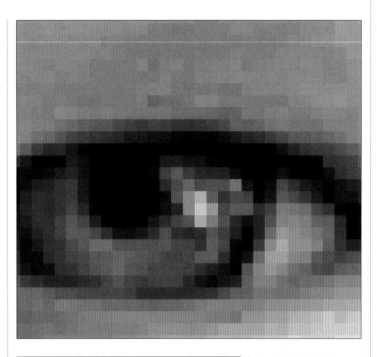

A portion of a digital image enlarged. At this magnification it's easy to see the individual pixels (picture elements) which make up the picture.

Open your image with picture editing software and you can summon a dialogue to determine how many of these pixels make up your image.

ESTIMATE TO ACCUMULATE

A pixel count provides a guide to the resolution of the camera and the pictures it will produce. However, some manufacturers use a software process known as 'interpolation' to increase the factor of resolution. Interpolation is a method by which more pixels appear in the picture than were actually captured by the camera. 'Real' pixels are examined and the camera's software guesses what a pixel which falls between them might look like. The new pixel is added to the image and the picture's pixel count grows accordingly.

Interpolation can result in pictures which have a resolution far in excess of that captured but, as you might imagine,

Although interpolation will fill in the rough gaps in a low-resolution picture, it cannot add true picture data where none exists. The results of interpolation are generally superior to the original image, but the effect remains visible.

the results of guessing what pixels look like can never equal images based on actual pixels. Interpolation was a commonplace technique in the days of VGA cameras, but hardware has advanced at such a pace that interpolated pixel counts are now only rarely quoted as a factor of resolution for digital cameras.

Interpolation is not a con, by the way, as long as it's clear to you that an interpolated resolution is not the same as *actual* resolution. Indeed, all good image editing software cleverly interpolates pixels once you enlarge an image beyond the resolution of the original; otherwise your enlargements would be pixelated.

supercomputer to its silicon knees), a digital representation of an analogue occurrence from the real world is never anything better than an approximation!

Elementary Pictures

If you've shopped for a digital camera, it's certain that you've encountered the word 'pixel'. Even if you have no idea what a pixel is, it probably became clear to you quite quickly that more is definitely better as far as pixels go, hence the buzzwords, 'megapixel' and 'multimegapixel'.

Pixel is another one of those contractions of words favoured in the hi-tech world and which, in this case, is a contraction of the words 'picture' and 'element.' Pixel refers to the smallest addressable element of a picture - that is, the smallest block of a picture that can be switched on or off to represent light and shade.

The earliest digital cameras provided a typical resolution of 320x240 pixels. An image at this resolution will appear crude and 'blocky' when viewed onscreen or printed, because there aren't enough pixels to fool the eye into seeing a 'continuous' flow of light and shade. Advances in technology soon led to cameras that were able to capture images at 640x480 pixels - matching the best in PC computer screen resolutions of the time. Images at this resolution appear

Examine the pictures below and you can see why buying a camera with the highest possible resolution is preferable. The images on the left were taken with a six megapixel camera (the close-up shows how the image decays under close scrutiny), while with the images on the right - taken with a twelve megapixel camera - even the close-up shows remarkably good resolution.

smooth onscreen but still look crude when printed, unless the picture is very small, say, 2 × 1.3 inches. Any bigger, and each pixel must be enlarged to the point at which it becomes clearly visible and the image is said to appear 'pixelated'.

By the late 1990s, the first megapixel cameras became available. These offered a height x width resolution that adds up to more than a million pixels. The introduction of megapixel cameras moved digital photography into the fast lane because images could at last be reproduced at the standard enprint (150x100mm) size, and yet be 'photorealistic' (supposedly indistinguishable from a real photograph).

Unless you're on a very tight budget

ALL-SEEING EYE?

Today's 'hobbyist' multimegapixel cameras offer resolutions of between 6 and 12 megapixels. The latest professional digital cameras can provide a staggering 39 million pixels per image. But the human eye has the equivalent of 230 million pixels, so digital cameras have some way to go yet!

or will only view your images onscreen, choose a camera with at least a six megapixel sensor. Today, even mid-range cameras offer multimegapixel resolution - between 6 and 8 million pixels - which is more than enough for quality prints and enlargements.

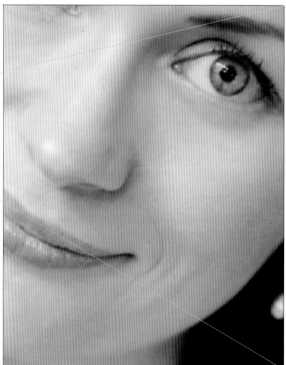

FILES AND FORMATS

As digital image capture and manipulation have evolved, so increasing numbers of formats in which to represent and store the results have become available. Each has its merits but all is not equal in the backing storage stakes.

Users of conventional cameras 'store' their pictures as negatives or transparencies. For digital camera users too, storing an image is a distinct step in the process of creating a picture - the image is captured and stored within the camera, possibly transferred to a computer as a picture file before being edited and printed. But the intermediate stage - storing the image as a file - is an important step, and a number of formats have been devised to store digital information as efficiently as possible.

It's this drive for efficiency and accuracy, however, which has caused so many file formats to be devised. Raw picture data takes up a relatively large space within your camera and so a certain amount of compression - squeezing of the image data - is applied in order to pack more pictures into the ever-limited 'backing storage' in the camera.

The Compression Problem

But compression isn't a cure-all, and many compression techniques result in degraded image quality. Some formats are rather less able than others, and which one you choose depends on your application - whether your pictures are intended to be viewed as prints or only in web pages, for example. Generally, file formats target one of two areas: colour accuracy at the expense of file size, or vice versa.

There are many file formats for storing digital images and each is geared to a particular application. GIFs, for example, are generally used for relatively low-resolution images intended for the Web, whereas the TIFF format is ideal for storing photorealistic pictures with high colour definition.

GIF

TIFF

The Formats

JPEG (pronounced 'jay-peg'): The most popular format for images taken with digital cameras today is the JPEG, and there's a good reason for this. JPEG is an acronym that stands for the (International Standards Organization's) Joint Photographic Experts Group, which created the format and devised it specifically for digital photographs. JPEG files offer 24-bit colour representation - that is, they can contain up to 16.7 million colours, which is more than enough for photorealistic pictures. Compression is high too resulting in small picture files (though size is relative in file formats) and the supreme advantage of the JPEG is that it only stores data for pixels that have colour - white pixels require no data.

The downside is that JPEGs use 'lossy' compression. Redundant picture information is actually discarded to reduce the file size. Obviously, throwing away information from the picture will degrade it. What's more, compression is applied every time the JPEG is opened and saved (though not when opened, viewed, and closed without saving).

GIF: The other major picture file format and certainly the most widespread on the Web is the GIF (Graphics Interchange Format). GIFs are ideal for 'portable' pictures that are likely to be viewed only on a computer screen (for example, those you want to post on a website). Compression is very high and generally the same picture rendered as a GIF will be far smaller than in any other format but at the expense of colour - GIF only allows a maximum of 250 colours.

JPEG, maximum quality   JPEG, maximum compression

Compression techniques enable you to store high-resolution images with a small cost in storage, but use with care as many compression systems are 'lossy' which means picture data is discarded in favour of file size.

TIFF: In professional publishing, the TIFF reigns supreme. TIFF (Tagged Image File Format) offers 16.7 million colours and uses a 'lossless' compression equation, which retains picture data, but results in files that are larger than some other compressed picture formats.

PNG: Newcomer PNG (Portable Network Group) is a Web-oriented format designed to retain picture integrity and produce small files. Lossless compression, 24-bit colour and meta-tags (indexing text for Web search engines contained within the picture) make the format ideal for Internet use.

FEATURE PACKED

All digital cameras come bristling with features, some of which you'll use every time you take a picture. Resolution is paramount, but LCD screens, self timers, and on-board special effects can make picture-taking more fun and ease you gently into the world of digital editing.

Between the writing and the reading of this book, prices for digital cameras will have fallen considerably and specifications increased significantly.

Until relatively recently, 640x480 pixels was considered a reasonable working resolution, and then along came affordable multimegapixel cameras, and now 640x480-pixel cameras are considered acceptable only for pictures intended for the Web. So if your idea of digital photography is as a replacement for a conventional camera and your pictures will be printed, a multimegapixel camera is a must.

Specifications

All digital cameras have a lens (fixed and plastic, in the case of cheaper offerings), viewfinder (low- and mid-range cameras are 'compacts', and the viewfinder is separate from the lens), and a body which houses the electronics and perhaps a removable storage option. Digital compact cameras are usually equipped with a lens that is the focal length equivalent of the 35mm to 50mm lens of a conventional 35mm film-based camera, and provide a field of view broadly comparable to the human eye.

The very cheapest cameras have a fixed-focus lens (don't confuse this with autofocus)

which, combined with aperture and shutter speed, will focus everything from about 1.5 metres to infinity. Most digital cameras offer autofocus and a macro facility for close-up pictures. Many better-quality cameras sport a zoom lens that novice photographers generally think of as a tool for getting closer to

This Fujifilm digital camera features a 28–300mm zoom lens, which will cover everything from wide angle landscape pictures to close up wildlife shots.

Shutter release button

Infrared focus

Function selector dial

Accessory shoe

Onboard flash

Lens

Manual zoom

Camera body

Exposure mode

Viewfinder mode

Viewfinder

Control wheel

LCD monitor

Multi selector

Display button

Menu button

Feature Packed

Digital Slideshow

Connectivity doesn't stop at linking your camera to a computer. Some cameras offer a 'video out' function, which enables you to connect the camera to a television set or VCR and view your pictures as a slideshow.

But the most obvious feature that sets the digital camera apart from its conventional cousin is an LCD screen for reviewing, editing, and deleting pictures, configuring the camera and selecting options. All but the cheapest cameras have an LCD, which can also double as a viewfinder. The LCD generally gives access to other features too, such as setting resolution, compression, and file type, and the result of applying an onboard effect, say, sepia toning, can also be viewed on the LCD screen.

The back of the same camera, showing its various control features, and above it, a typical control panel. These indicate battery life, file format, exposure, macro, red-eye, and flash settings, among other things.

distant action. However, the zoom lens is more useful as a framing device, letting the photographer remain outside the 'personal space' of the subject.

All digital cameras can download pictures to a computer. Early examples were equipped with a serial connector, but this has been replaced by USB (Universal Serial Bus). USB is hot-swappable so the computer recognises your camera as soon as it's connected and launches the appropriate software. The latest version (USB 2.0 Hi-Speed) is much faster than USB 1.0 or USB 2.0 'Full Speed' connections.

More recently, FireWire has become available, with a FireWire port built into the majority of PC models.

CONSUMER CHOICE

Digital camera manufacturers fall into two camps: those from traditional camera companies such as Nikon, Canon, and Olympus, and those from companies that are principally involved in the manufacture of consumer electronic goods, and which make everything from computers to microwave ovens (Sanyo, Samsung, Hewlett-Packard, and Casio). The traditional camera manufacturers tend to produce digital examples that are familiar in size, shape, and operation to anyone who has used a conventional camera, whereas the latter group often approach digital camera manufacture in more novel and interesting ways. Take each on merit and make your choice on features and price.

DIGITAL STORAGE

So you thought you'd seen the last of film? Think again! Just as conventional cameras require conventional film, digital cameras need digital 'film', but the advantage is that it can be used time and time again.

Digital pictures are big! A high-resolution photograph might require as much as 5 or 6 megabytes (MB) of storage within the camera. The first digital cameras had fixed internal storage that was gradually filled as pictures were taken. When the camera was 'full', the pictures had to be transferred to a computer or erased. Today's multimegapixel cameras produce images at stupendous resolutions, and with truly enormous file sizes as a result. Not for them the fixed internal storage scheme. Instead, storage cards - 'digital film' - are used. Typically, manufacturers have thrown their weight behind competing formats. The popular cards are for the most part standard memory cards, such as might be found in an electronic organiser. Making use of removable cards enables photographers to keep spares in their camera case and plug in a fresh one when necessary. Of course, there's nothing remotely like conventional film within the case of the card. It is simply an electronic device which features memory chips and a means by which information can be stored and retrieved.

The End of Floppies

For a time, Sony persevered with cameras that used floppy disks as their storage medium. The cameras were slightly cumbersome, but the floppy disks made a lot of sense. They're cheap, widely available, portable, and reliable. However, the advent of megapixel cameras and large picture files spelled the end for the floppy. What's more, economies of scale equate to ever-cheaper storage cards as digital cameras become more widespread.

At present, two major contenders vie for your camera's card slot: CompactFlash and SD (Secure Digital). It used to be the case that CompactFlash was used in digital SLR cameras,

SD cards *(right)* are cheap, readily available, and tiny, which means you can carry spares for those outings where you intend to take a lot of pictures.

Memory cards are available in generic formats such as the CompactFlash card *(right, above)* or more proprietary formats such as the xD Picture Card *(right, below).*

CAPACITY			
SIZE OF CARD	**NUMBER OF IMAGES**		
	Best JPEG (8MP camera)	Best JPEG (10MP camera)	Best JPEG (12MP camera)
128MB	30	25	20
256MB	60	50	40
512MB	120	100	80
1GB	240	200	160
2GB	490	410	330

and SD cards in digital compacts. In recent years many camera makers have switched to SD in their digital SLR cameras as well. SD cards are smaller (so the camera can be made smaller) and the latest SDHC (High Capacity) cards are now available in capacities up to 4GB (gigabytes), which means you have plenty of space for pictures. Only the newest cameras will take SDHC cards though.

Despite the name, CompactFlash cards are physically larger than SD ones, but still offer greater storage space - up to 8GB - but these cards now tend to be the domain of professional cameras.

Proprietary Cards

Sony offers a proprietary card called a 'Memory Stick', which can be used in other Sony equipment like camcorders, MP3 players and games consoles. This is great if you have a number of compatible gadgets, but there are so many variations it's easy to get confused and they also can't be used in non-Sony cameras.

Olympus and Fujifilm also developed their own memory card format - the xD Picture Card - which is the smallest memory card type on the market. Most Olympus and Fujifilm compacts will use this card, although some will also let you use another card type (SD or CompactFlash) as well.

Sony's Memory Stick is a proprietary format that is relatively expensive when compared with CompactFlash and SD. It can, however, be used in other Sony products, which might mean a saving if you're already a user or a fan!

MAKE THE CONNECTION

Taking a picture is just the first step – you must get the image into your computer and printer before it becomes the print that your friends and relatives would recognise as a photograph.

All digital cameras are equipped with a means by which they can be connected to a computer, so that you can transfer your pictures for storage, manipulation, printing, emailing, and so on. The most common connection you'll find is USB (Universal Serial Bus) which has been universally adopted and is available in several speeds.

Universally Superior

In the mid-1990s, some of the major players in the computer world got together to establish a new 'standard' for serial connections. Compaq, DEC, IBM, Intel, Microsoft, and others created the Universal Serial Bus (USB). USB is 'hot-swappable', which means that when you attach a camera, the computer knows it's connected, automatically invokes the necessary software and establishes a link. You don't have to switch off, reboot, or manually launch software.

All new PCs over the past couple of years (and certainly all brand new ones) have at least one or more USB ports, as do Apple Macs, and USB is standard across platforms - the same cables work with any machine that has USB ports. The connectors themselves are small and easy to use.

As the technology developed USB 2.0

appeared, which is available in 'Full Speed' and 'Hi-Speed' versions. Hi-Speed is the faster connection and unless a camera or other computer accessory specifically says it's Hi-Speed then it will be Full Speed - even though both are confusingly called USB 2.0.

Fly by Wire

Not for nothing is Apple a leader in the professional media world. In 1995 the company launched a n ew serial transfer scheme known as 'FireWire'. Capable of truly blistering transfer speeds (400 megabits per second (Mbps), compared with USB's 12Mbps), FireWire languished for a time as a poor second to USB because no suitable

When you connect your camera to your computer, the screen will tell you that you have 'created' another drive (i.e., your camera) and will list the files (your pictures) on that drive.

WHAT'S IN A NAME?

In computer speak, a data connector on a computer is known as a 'port'.

Camera

Computer

Printer

Camera

Printer

Although it's entirely possible to use and enjoy a digital camera without going anywhere near a computer, you'll be able to get far more from your images by transferring them to a Mac or PC. A computer makes an excellent storage medium for all that image data too.

application existed. Then Sony included a FireWire port on its newly launched digital video camera, and suddenly the potential for FireWire became clear. Where digital photographs produce large files, digital video generates memory-defying files of breathtaking proportions. Transferring them required the incredible muscle of FireWire. All G4 Apple Macintosh computers had these ports, and so do almost all new PCs and Macs. FireWire is generally reserved for high-end multimegapixel professional digital cameras, which generate large file sizes.

A new addition is FireWire 800, which, as the name suggests, has an 800 megabits per second data transfer rate - double that of the original FireWire connection. As a result, the older version is now referred to as FireWire 400. It's important to note that the two 'plug sockets' for FireWire are different, so FireWire 800 devices won't plug into FireWire 400 computers.

A Wireless Future?

A number of new cameras now come equipped with a 'wireless' connection, so you don't need to hunt around for cables to connect your camera to your computer. This is a technology that is still in its infancy in mass-market cameras, although it has been around for a while in the world

of professional photography - especially sports photography. Here, the camera can be fired using a remote control and it will automatically (and wirelessly) send the images to the photographer's laptop computer, or even straight to a newspaper picture desk. As a result the photographer can put their camera behind a goal or on the touchline where they couldn't otherwise stand.

Simple versions of wireless (WiFi) control are now appearing in digital compact cameras too, so you can sit and view images on the TV in your living room while the camera 'zaps' them to your computer where they can be stored. It's slower than transferring them using USB or FireWire, but much more convenient than finding the right cable!

Computers provide connectors ('ports') and various software protocols to enable users to transfer data. Slow connections such as bi-directional parallel and serial ports have now been replaced by USB and FireWire.

WHICH PORT IN A STORM?

Ethernet

USB

FireWire 400

WHICH COMPUTER?

Though it isn't absolutely necessary, chances are you'll want to connect your camera to a computer to store, edit, and print your pictures. Two distinct types of computer dominate the marketplace, and which you choose depends on a number of factors.

'No-one ever got fired for buying IBM,' ran the advertising slogan, and in the early 1980s it was true. IBM's personal desktop computer (as opposed to the mini and mainframe computers that IBM also manufactured back then) quickly came to dominate the market; and in the PC's wake followed an avalanche of clones. Indeed, so successful were these lookalike computers that sales of them eventually exceeded those of IBM, and PC-compatible manufacturers such as Compaq ousted IBM as the number-one sellers.

PC Versus Mac

When it was launched, the PC came with a command-line driven operating system (that is, you typed in obscure commands such as DIR, DEL, MD, and so on) created by a little-known Seattle software company called Microsoft. Then Apple launched its Macintosh computer, which featured the world's first truly commercial point-and-click graphic interface. 'Windows', icons, a mouse, and pointers passed into common currency, and Microsoft wanted its share. The Seattle company launched Windows, which was treated as something of a joke for several years in its earlier guises. However, with the launch of Windows 95,

Microsoft hit paydirt and computer users around the globe bought and installed the system, while Apple failed to license its own products to other developers (its key error).

So successful is Microsoft's system that today a PC and a Windows computer are generally thought of as one and the same thing. However, publishing professionals use the Apple computer almost exclusively, and with the launch of the PowerPC and then the iMac, Apple began to claw back respectable

Although a computer is a welcome friend in the digital darkroom, there's no need to plump for large and ugly boxes! Today's PCs *(above)* and Macs *(top)* are aesthetically pleasing in their own right.

market share. Which one you choose - PC or Mac - depends on who you are and what you want to do. If digital photography is a pastime, and your pictures will be stored on a computer that is also shared with your family, it's almost certain that you'll choose (or probably already own) a PC.

A Very PC Solution

PCs are generally cheaper than Macs and more widely available. All PCs use off-the-shelf plug-in components that are easily swapped when repairs are required, there's a wealth of quality software of all kinds to support the machine, and finding help is as easy as asking a friend or work colleague - every second person is familiar with PCs and Windows.

The Mac, on the other hand, remains relatively unknown outside pro-media circles, although the latest Intel Macs have changed that to an extent - they can run both the Macintosh operating system and Windows. Macs offer excellent graphic options as standard across the platform (no grappling with video driver software from third-party graphic card suppliers), a robust operating system, which is arguably better integrated, smoother, and more intuitive than Windows, and some very high-quality, image-manipulation software, some of which can be found nowhere else.

All new Macs and PCs feature plenty of RAM, large hard drives and fast processors; each offers USB ports as standard and almost all have FireWire, and each provides access to CD and DVD writers, easy Internet access, and a lot more to broaden your horizon.

SOFT OPTIONS

Though a comparatively large investment, a computer is simply the means to an end: using image-editing software. This software is a primary reason why digital photography is so much fun. Once the pictures in your camera are transferred to your computer, image-editing software enables you to view and manipulate them in ways that previously required an entire darkroom's worth of expensive equipment and years of experience. Image editors are available in many guises, some aimed at beginners, some at media professionals. Prices vary enormously too, from free (that is bundled with the camera) to hundreds of pounds. However, software is one of the few products about which 'you get what you pay for' can't be said. A relatively cheap image editor such as Corel's Paint Shop Pro for the PC is packed with features, it's easy to use, and you can download a try-then-buy version from the Internet before actually spending your money. At the other end of the scale, Adobe Photoshop has every feature imaginable and is available for both PC and Mac - but at a hefty professional price!

Hardware

SILICON-FREE PHOTOGRAPHY

Digital photography means 'instant' pictures and no more processing costs. You've side-stepped film, but have you had to acquire a computer instead? And what are the options if you don't own a computer?

Don't let the lack of a computer put you off buying and using a digital camera. Computers have certainly entered millions of homes over the past 10 years or so, but not everyone owns one. Just because you're a digital photographer doesn't mean you want to be a computer programmer too!

Computer or Printer?

Of course, the first thing to realise is that manipulating digital images calls for as much or as little technical expertise as you're willing to acquire. With no more knowledge of computers than switching them on and plugging in cables, you can download your pictures and save them to disk. A chapter or two of this book, and half a day invested in experimenting, and you'll be cropping, re-sizing, and toning your pictures, burning CD picture albums, and sending images to friends over the Internet like an old hand; and after that, the digital darkroom is yours to command.

But let's assume for a moment that you don't have a computer, and prefer instead to invest in the best camera your money can buy. Back to that 'household penetration'

quotient. You might not have a computer, but it's certain that a relative or a friend has one, and while they probably won't want you spending hours poring over their machines with your pictures, an hour here and there while you download them and file them to a CD ought to be okay.

Orphans who shun friendship aren't altogether stymied either. Those who work usually come into contact with computers, those who don't can probably gain access to silicon at a public library, and students of all

If you don't have space for a full-sized desktop computer, consider a laptop. These have the processing power of many desktop machines in a compact and convenient format. Be aware that you'll pay more for equivalent features than you would for a desktop PC.

ages can petition their schools and colleges for time on a machine (but always remember to ask permission before you make free with someone's computer).

In the Hand

If not owning a computer is an issue of space, consider a palmtop or laptop. These handheld and portable computers offer processor speeds, hard-drive space, and RAM memory that's on a par with the desktop computers, but they occupy far less space. All will enable you to connect to the Internet too, so you can post your pictures (that is, insert them into a webpage) or send them to others via email. Despite their convenience and incredible miniature technology, palmtops and laptops are not that much more expensive than a comparable desktop computer, and have many advantages. There are also good deals to be had on second-user and end-of-line machines.

Your Prints Will Come

Those who truly don't want a computer of any sort don't have to have one. Many inkjet printers sport a built-in card slot as standard. Fill your camera with pictures, withdraw the storage card, plug it into the printer's slot, select from a range of printing options on the printer's LCD menu panel (enlargements and reductions, colour or mono output, and so on), and go ahead and print. You'll get good results, and all without a computer. And many cameras offer basic editing features right in the camera so you can even crop and compose your pictures before printing them.

Shop Smart

Some conventional photography outlets and pharmacies also provide a print-from-card option. Take your pictures as before, eject the card, and pop it along to the store much as you would a conventional film. The result is a package of prints and an empty card ready to use again.

With no printer *(above)*, you can take your digital camera storage card to a high street processing outlet (almost all conventional camera and film outlets offer this service). Alternatively, you can email your image files to an online processor *(below)*. It's easy!

3

Point and Click

The world of photography is littered with casualties! There are no bandages or medicines and the only bruising is an ego or two, but they are casualties nonetheless, as the small ads of photography magazines fill up with hi-tech camera equipment, sold off cheaply as people's interest wanes. Why does it happen? Because the wise photographer realises that a top-of-the-range digital camera can produce Box Brownie pictures in the 'wrong' hands. And what are the wrong hands? Those that skip this chapter, which contains old - it's true! - but exceedingly valuable advice for budding picture-takers. Covered here is composition, lighting, positioning, and the half dozen or so other techniques which, while simple in themselves, turn good photographs into great ones.

GROUNDWORK

The basic rules of photography exist to guide and hone your talent, not to stifle it. Learning and mastering these simple techniques will equip you with all that's required for truly gorgeous pictures – the rest is up to you.

Guitar players spend much of their time worrying about whether learning to read music will spoil their musical intuition - that indefinable 'something' that ensures their playing is inspired. It's a worry that could apply equally to photographers. After all, many of the world's most famous images were taken on the hoof with little regard for the rules of composition and lighting, or these rules were abandoned on purpose to create a particular effect.

But what conclusion have seasoned guitarists and photographers reached? That to throw away the rule book, you have to have one first! It's a cliché but it's true, the best camera in the world won't make you Diane Arbus or David Bailey, but the cheapest disposable compact would enable either photographer to produce marvellous pictures. Photography is about looking and seeing, and good photography is about composition, balance, lighting, and tone.

Composing

Arguably, the principal factor that sets an interesting picture apart from a dull one is composition - not the subject itself, but the way in which you choose to present it.

Whether as a journalistic record of an event or an artistic representation of what you see, the appeal of any photograph can be strengthened by training your eye to see a composed picture. When you survey a scene your eyes take in everything and your brain picks out what it perceives as the important details. The camera, however, isolates just one part of the scene, framing and flattening it into a two-dimensional representation that can be dramatically different from the way you perceived it.

The 'rule' might be expressed as: don't aim, frame. Build a picture rather than simply point

A common mistake is to position the strongest point of interest at the center of the picture. Add greater impact by composing your picture using the 'rule of thirds,' an age-old technique designed to build in balance and add drama.

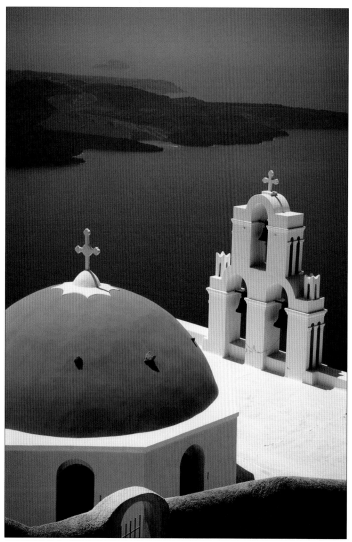

The seasons have a great impact on light quality and availability. In the winter months, stark reflected light from snow will tend to fool your camera's metering system, and the result could be a poor exposure.

the camera. Assess the scene and decide where its interesting highlights lie. Allow your eye time to scan the subject in the viewfinder. If you're unsure, use the LCD screen to supplement the framing. Practise observing what's around you as potential pictures, isolating and framing portions to make subjects. Of course, the advantage of a digital camera is that you can take a picture many times while you practise this technique without wasting film.

Lighting Effects

Second only to composition is lighting. Stark lighting (such as strong flash) can have a very dramatic effect, especially in portraiture, by stripping a subject of personal space, while sympathetic soft or natural light enhances and is kind to subjects. Low-key lighting suggests reflective moods, while high-key lighting, and lighting filters and effects, can produce a party atmosphere. Although your eye might not notice it, the time of day, seasons, and weather all have a significant effect on light. Try setting your camera on a tripod and taking the same exposure at two-hourly intervals throughout the day - the difference in light is dramatic.

Balance is important to composition. Ensure the horizon is level and alter your vantage point so you can build surrounding features into the picture to support the composition.

GET A GRIP

Holding your camera, tilting and twisting it, getting up high, or crouching low – all have a significant impact on your pictures, and form the basic techniques for creating more dramatic photographs.

It's likely that your digital camera is what's known as a 'compact.' Unlike a single-lens reflex (SLR), which uses the same lens to view and take the picture, the compact's lens and finder are separate - you look through one and capture the scene with the other. The system works perfectly well (indeed, some of the world's most famous photographs were taken using rangefinder cameras - a variation on the compact theme), but there is potential for problems. The most obvious is that you leave on the lens cap or otherwise obscure its view with a finger without realising.

Learning to handle and hold your camera will help you to avoid these simple problems. Of course, with a digital camera, obscuring your picture with a finger or the lens cap costs only time and effort while you erase the

Interesting vantage points breathe life into your photographs. Look for shapes and textures to catch the eye and engage the interest of all who see your pictures. Here, the gutter between these glorious roof tiles leads the eye into the picture.

picture and make another exposure - there's no film to waste, and you're aware of the problem immediately. But where you are in relation to your subject matter is what will turn a good picture into a great one!

Handheld

Hold your camera with a firm but gentle grip. The shutter release will almost certainly be positioned on the right of the camera, so whether you're right or left-handed, cup the camera snugly in the palm of your left hand and curl the fingers of your right hand around its right-hand edge so that your index finger falls naturally over the shutter button - the classic landscape position. Keep your elbows tucked in and your feet slightly apart. Simply turn the camera through 90 degrees for a portrait format. Held like this, the camera will be largely immune from shake (and blurred pictures) and your fingers are out of the way.

Getting above your subject adds perspective, depth, and drama, and will enable you to frame more effectively - especially with a group portrait such as a wedding picture or a sporting event - and crop out unwanted detail. Effort made at this stage of the picture will reduce the work required during the editing process.

The Lowdown

Children are smaller than adults, and so are family pets, yet so many pictures of kids and animals are taken looking down at them. Better by far to get down low where you can see the world the way they see it.

Up Close

Enlarging digital images is easy, but it has a cost in resolution. How many times have you seen or taken pictures which lacked impact because the point of interest in the picture was a little blob in one corner? Getting in close to your subject will tease out the interesting aspects, and produce appealing pictures.

Never work with children and animals... unless you can get down to their eye view. Seeing what this kitten sees provides a view of its world rather than yours, in what might otherwise be an ordinary picture.

VITAL STATISTICS

Aperture, shutter speed, and focal length are a camera's vital ingredients, and each combines to produce your picture. The same is true of digital cameras, though the way these are expressed can be different.

An exposure is the result of two factors: the speed at which the camera's shutter opens and closes; and the width of the aperture through which light passes. The same is true whether you're using a conventional or digital camera. Shutter speeds are usually measured in fractions of a second: 1/30th, 1/60th, 1/125th, 1/250th, 1/500th. Aperture is measured in f-stops: f/2, f/4, f/5.6, f/8, f/16. Each stop admits half the light of the previous setting.

A slow shutter speed allows more time for the light that is passing through the aperture to reach the CCD. Similarly, a wider aperture allows more light to pass through. It follows that combinations of the two enable the same amount of light to reach the CCD.

With many mid- to high-end digital cameras, the photographer has complete control over the way these two factors are combined to produce a picture, and all but the most basic digital cameras offer some degree of control. The question is, why and when to favour aperture over shutter, or shutter over aperture? The answer lies in depth of field and

The result of incorrectly combining aperture and shutter speed is an under- or overexposed picture. It's possible to compensate for poor exposures using image editing software, but, inevitably, detail will be lost (crucial when working with a finite number of pixels).

Correct exposure

Underexposed

Overexposed

movement. A narrow aperture allows more of the picture to be in focus. That is, a picture exposed at 1/60th of a second and f/16 will focus everything between a yard and infinity (described as 'depth of field'), which is ideal for landscapes. But 1/60th is slow, and if there's movement in the scene, it could be blurred.

Light, Camera... Action!

So when taking an 'action' photo a fast shutter speed of say, 1/500th of a second, and a correspondingly wider aperture of perhaps f/2.8 are used. This lets enough light enter the camera for your subject to be in focus, while other details will be blurred.

What does all this mean to digital cameras, which have a CCD rather than a shutter? Much

Looking out over vegetation, a narrow aperture and slow shutter speed keep everything in focus, and is an ideal combination when photographing a landscape.

MISSING LINK

Electronic metering may be thought of as the missing link between conventional and digital cameras. In the 1970s, manufacturers extended the idea of a built-in exposure meter by linking it directly to electronics controlling the camera's aperture and shutter. The camera measured the light, and set either the shutter or aperture to suit the manual setting of the other. These are known as 'aperture-priority' and 'shutter-priority' modes, because the photographer chooses one to suit the scene and the camera selects the other.

the same. A digital camera fired at 1/500th of a second makes an exposure just like a conventional camera. The difference is that the CCD is turned on and off for 1/500th of a second rather than the plates of a shutter passing across a film frame. The control you have over the aperture settings of digital cameras depends on the camera. Mid-range cameras allow manual aperture settings, but most have a 'motion' setting for taking action photographs.

A wide aperture allows effects such as 'panning.' The camera is focused before the subject appears and the camera is moved as it sweeps through the scene while the shutter is released. The out-of-focus background gives a dramatic indication of speed.

CLEAR AND CLOSE UP

A blurred image can provide dramatic impact, but more usually your aim will be to capture scenes in perfect focus – which is especially important when working within the finite resolution of a digital camera.

On the previous pages you learned that focusing is as much a factor of aperture as it is of dialling in the correct distance between the lens and its subject. When light passes through a narrow aperture, it undergoes a kind of 'natural' focusing. This property enables camera manufacturers to build cameras that are described as being fixed-focus - there is no way to change the focusing distance of the lens. Instead, a relatively slow shutter speed is combined with a narrow aperture to ensure that on sunny days or when using flash, everything between about 4 feet and infinity will be more or less in focus. Fixed-focus cameras are cheap and work, but they're creatively limiting.

Ghostly Images

Manual focus cameras - generally either rangefinders and SLR types - rely on the photographer to set the lens to the correct distance between camera and subject. This is achieved with the aid of a focusing tool rather than by measuring or guessing. Rangefinder cameras resemble compacts in that they have a separate lens and viewfinder, but these two lenses are linked in such a way that turning the distance ring on the lens causes a 'ghost' image in the viewfinder to move. When the ghost image and main viewfinder image are aligned - the one transposed over the top of the other - the lens is focused.

SLRs generally offer a combination of aids such as a split screen and a fresnel screen. The split screen shows a divided image which is aligned as the lens is focused. When the divided image joins up, the lens is in focus. A fresnel screen resembles a pixelated digital image which is made to grow gradually less pixelated as the lens is brought into focus. The fresnel screen is used widely with twin-lens reflex cameras.

During the 1980s, autofocusing became widely available. As you squeeze the shutter button, the camera fires an infrared (or occasionally a sonic) beam at the subject which is reflected back to the camera. The distance is calculated from the delay between sending and receiving and the shutter focused accordingly. All mid-range digital cameras feature autofocus as standard. Professional cameras

Autofocus cameras fire an infrared beam at the subject, which is then reflected back to the camera, letting its onboard sensors judge the distance and pull the lens into focus accordingly.

often feature a manual override to enable experienced photographers to choose.

Though autofocus works well, there is a small delay between pressing the shutter, focusing the camera, and the shutter firing. This can be a problem if you're trying to capture a moving target but there is a way around it known as 'locking' the focus. Aim the camera at something which is at a similar distance, squeeze the shutter to focus the camera and hold the shutter button. You can now recompose the picture and fire the shutter at the required time. You can also use this method to focus on subjects outside the centre of the frame, by pointing the camera momentarily away while you focus, then back again to take the picture.

UP CLOSE AND PERSONAL

Zooming is one of those gimmicks that camera and lens manufacturers make much of because they know that getting close to the action holds an immeasurable appeal for novice photographers. However, unlike some gimmicks, zooming offers many possibilities. Certainly you can 'get closer' to distant subjects, but the real value lies in the way a zoomed lens tends to flatten depth of field, tightly packing the 'layers' of a scene. This flattening effect is perfect for portraiture because it flatters the subject, and enables the photographer to get in close without making the model uncomfortable. Perhaps most importantly, zooming helps you to fill the frame with the subject, lending greater impact, and helping to avoid the classic mistake of cluttered pictures with what should be the point of interest lost in a corner.

Used even on a landscape picture, zooming in on a detail - such as this almost human-looking rock formation - flattens the background and adds impact to the subject to create a striking image.

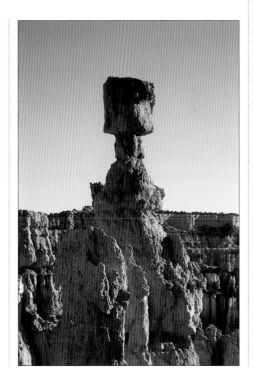

DIGITAL COLOUR

During its early years photography was a monochrome process and colour was the Holy Grail. But the advent of colour processing brought with it the realisation that black-and-white photographs can be every bit as striking.

Colour stirs the emotions in a way that transcends the relative simplicity of composition and technical application. Colour can convey tension, it can comfort, it can inform, or it can be simply abstract, the artistic value of the picture derived from the combination of colours within and the subject itself without recognisable form. Paradoxically, where colour can convey emotion, a lack of colour can have an equally potent effect. Used carefully, a greyscale treatment will bring great beauty and impact to an image.

Colour Variations

It's important to realise at the outset that in photography there is no true colour. The same scene shot at the same time with the same camera, but on different film, will result in photographs that are very different tonally. Digital cameras vary even more so. Manufacturers tend to weight one colour over another and by its very nature the digital process itself is incapable of anything more than an approximation (albeit a pretty good one!) of the range of colours in a scene. Though 24-bit colour offers a remarkable palette of more than 16 million hues, the human eye can distinguish almost infinitely subtle variations which can be

This scene is brought to life by the availability of colour which gives reason to the composition and delights the eye.

lost in a digital sample. Time of day, the seasons, and artificial lighting all have an impact too.

Some digital cameras provide a white-balance option as a counter to the colour

COMPLEMENTARY COLOURS

Colour is the result of mixing one or more hues. Where there are no hues the result is black, and all hues together are white. To represent this mixture artificially, on the printed page, for example, or on a television screen, several colour 'models' have been devised and two are used most frequently: RGB and CMYK. RGB stands for the primary colours red, green, and blue, and mixtures of these in various degrees make the other colours. RGB is used for television and computer screens, cameras, scanners, and binary devices. The CMYK model (which stands for cyan, magenta, yellow, and key plate - the plate that carries the black) is used for colour printing. This model is used because ink cannot reproduce the range of colours provided by the simpler, but tonally more subtle, RGB model.

Fortunately, when you come to print your RGB digital image, it is converted to CMYK colour automatically by the image-editing software or the printer's firmware (which accounts for the differences in the printed and onscreen image). RGB is said to be an 'additive' model because the colours are added together to create others. CMYK is a 'subtractive' model, as the colours are removed by degrees to provide the required hue.

(above) If your camera provides red and yellow filters, they can be used to powerful effect in black-and-white photographs. In this image a red filter has deepened the contrast between sky and clouds

(right) Colour conveys information which, though important, is sometimes second to mood, as in this scene. The greyscale and added noise give a gritty realism to the picture.

casting that artificial light can create. Some cameras offer red and yellow filters which profoundly affect the tones of black-and-white photographs. However, these effects can be simulated using image-editing software.

QUICK AS A FLASH

Light is your medium, but working with light can tax even the professionals. Too much and a picture's detail disappears into uniform whiteness, while too little and there is no photograph. Your aim is to balance the available light to build your pictures, to create highlights, mood, and tone.

All but the very cheapest, fixed-focus digital cameras sport a flash unit. But it's fair to say that these usually tiny electronic flash systems are often underpowered and the results when using them disappoint many digital photographers. The unit is charging from tiny batteries which are also powering the camera. You can expect a built-in flash unit on a compact camera to have a maximum working distance of about fifteen feet. The manual that accompanies your camera will tell you the unit's working distance.

Most digital cameras offer several flash modes: autoflash, in which the camera

Night photography can produce beautiful results, but you must mount the camera securely to avoid the blurring that is inevitable with the long exposures required.

(left) The bane of low-light photography (when pupils are wider to admit more light), red-eye occurs when flash is reflected from the retina at the back of the eye. Many cameras offer a red-eye reduction flash mode which fires the flash fractionally ahead of the shutter so that the subject's pupils contract before the picture is taken and red-eye is avoided *(left image)*.

Fill-in flash helps to light a subject that would otherwise be underexposed and lacking detail. This is when flash comes into its own.

decides whether to deploy the flash unit based on the exposure reading; and flash always on or always off. Switching on the flash yourself is useful when you need to light a subject that might otherwise be underexposed or thrown into silhouette, such as when shooting into bright light (this is known as 'fill-in' flash). In these circumstances the camera's exposure meter reading would almost certainly indicate that flash wasn't required. Switching off the flash is necessary if you want to take timed exposures - at night, for example - with the camera mounted on a tripod and using a very long exposure.

Reflected Glory

Wherever possible, make the most of available natural light. If your camera's metering tells you that flash is required, try using a reflector (a large piece of white card will do) to direct light onto your subject. A reflector placed horizontally beneath a head-and-shoulders portrait will direct light up into the face, softening shadows, smoothing wrinkles, and minimising prominent features. Close-ups work better with reflectors too where flash might burn out detail. Indoors, position your subject near a window (one that admits indirect light), so that your back and the subject's face is turned to the light.

Blocking Noise

Outdoors, shoot your pictures mid-morning or mid-afternoon to avoid the deep shadows thrown by the overhead midday sun. In dim light use a tripod or position the camera firmly on a steady surface and use the timer to fire the shutter and avoid camera shake. Though digital cameras generally work well at long exposure times, some "noise" will begin to creep into the picture, though you can use fill-in flash to avoid it. If the camera features an EV option, use it to expose backlit scenes correctly in which the point of interest might otherwise be silhouetted or when shooting in artificial lighting conditions.

THE HUMAN EXPERIENCE

Photographing people makes for an inexhaustible supply of potential subjects, and the picture-taking starts right in the home with family and friends. With a new camera, a fresh set of batteries, and an empty data storage card you have the potential for some truly great people pictures.

People are endlessly fascinating, and pictures of people provide a truly irresistible fascination. Our brains are 'trained' from childhood to recognise faces, to pick friendly or familiar faces from crowds, and to make a connection with faces and human form that is without parallel. For photographers, people provide an inexhaustible supply of material for interesting pictures, and for most of us that means we can find fantastic photos without even leaving the house. A good portrait picture preserves the moment enabling us to see beyond the obvious form and somehow glimpse the essence of a subject - though it's fair to say that the subject may not always like being preserved!

Pose the Question

During photography's early years, portraits were necessarily formal. Long exposure times required sitters to remain quite still for several minutes or more, effectively ruling out candid photography. The introduction of the Leica 35mm 'miniature' and similar small cameras freed the photographer from the formal subject, and allowed pictures to be taken in all kinds of interesting situations. Candid shots - those without the subject's knowledge - are explored elsewhere on these pages, but there is a mode of photography which falls between the rigidity of 'formal' and the voyeur-like approach of the unobserved and more 'candid' shot.

Informal pictures capture people in natural poses - which may or may not in fact be rigidly posed by you. A storekeeper leaning over the counter, a traffic policeman

Formal or informal, a portrait is a magnet for the eye. You want to see what, why, and when, who and where. Carry your camera and look for the moment that defines an experience, one in which the subject is contextualised within the confines of the image. It isn't easy and you'll discard far more images than you'll keep, but when it happens, you know you've got a great picture.

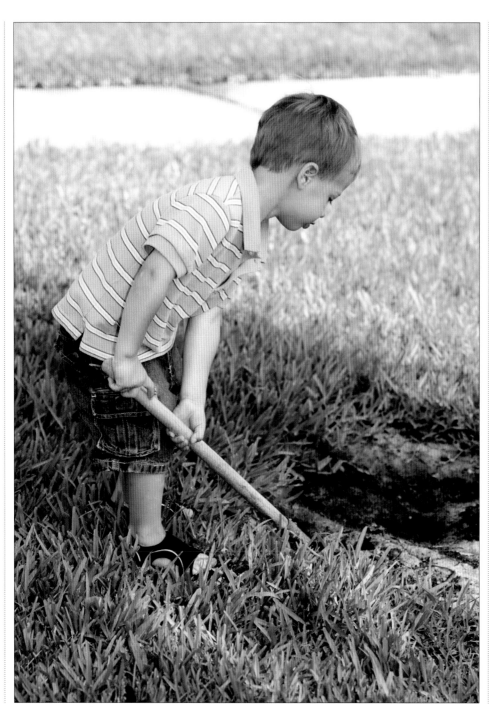

Children are endlessly fascinated by their world and it's that interaction with what's around them that makes for a compelling image - we want to know what it is the boy is about to dig up. Take lots of pictures of your kids so they become impervious to the camera and let you capture the moment.

caught mid-gesture, the sentry in his box, family pictures of people sitting at the kitchen table, on sofas, or enjoying the deck all reveal something about the subject which is at once interesting and compelling.

Even today, when the majority of people are completely familiar with the camera, it remains relatively difficult to capture people at ease. They become edgy and nervous, unable to relax, or else wooden and stiff. Give your subject something to do to focus their mind away from the camera. A prop is a good way to help relax your sitter, so suggest they hold a book, stroke a cat, or something similar.

If you're photographing someone who isn't sitting for you, side-step potential hostility and ask permission! Most people will agree after a token show of objecting. By gaining

Proof that a snap of a family group for the album can be every bit as interesting as the 'art' shot. Here the people are arranged in such a way that the eye is drawn into the picture. Height in the arrangement also plays a part and creates interest.

permission you can direct the subject into a 'pose' that justifies your interest.

If you're taking a holiay picture of a friend posed alongside a landmark, try to create distance, and work up some drama between the two. Use the widest setting on the lens, move far enough away from the landmark so that it isn't cropped, and stand the subject close to the camera. This will provide depth and enable both the person and the landmark to create their own space within the picture. Alternatively, keep your camera primed and take the picture when your subject is animated, but with the landmark as a back-drop - effectively a frame - to the movement. Use depth of field and selective focusing (a technique described elsewhere in this book) to draw out your subject.

Eye to Eye

There is no greater impact than that of the subject making eye contact with the photographer. The effect can be dramatic, poignant, inviting, or starkly rebuffing, but you can be sure that those who see the picture will feel the impact whatever its apparent message.

Ask the subject to look directly at the camera. This might be difficult if your subject is self-conscious and shy, and even those who aren't will find it difficult to stare into the lens for longer than a few moments. You can overcome the problem by speaking to the subject just before you fire the shutter, asking again for them to look at the camera, or you can capture their attention by making a noise or saying something unexpected.

If a face forms part of your picture and unless you're after a particular effect, always focus the lens on the eyes for maximum impact. Looking into the lens doesn't necessarily mean the subject should smile (though a glare might not be what you're looking for either). Try to determine what it is about your subject that you and others might find interesting and arrange the face to tease out that particular element.

When palm-sized cameras became a reality in the 1930s, all kinds of truly amazing

Get up close when taking portraits and fill your image with the subjects (or crop closely). There's nothing worse than squinting to make out a tiny pair of figures way off in one corner of the picture!

TWICE THE PICTURE

Here's a tip for a tense subject. Take a picture but then, immediately the subject relaxes (because the moment has passed), take another picture. This second one could well be the picture you imagined in the first place.

pictures were taken of the rich, famous (and infamous)! Where people were familiar with, and aware of photographers lumbering about with unwieldy box cameras, they were caught off-guard by the new wave of photographers shooting candid pictures.

The Name is Bond...

Today the same is true. Your digital camera is probably smaller again than any conventional device you've previously owned. What's more, it'll either be silent, or can be silenced at the touch of a button. The potential for candid pictures is immense!

The first rule of candid picture-taking is simply to let you and your camera become familiar. If you're almost invariably seen holding a camera, no one will think twice when you use it, thereby enabling you to capture the moment.

If you find yourself in a one-off situation where familiarity isn't an option, then try using various blinds: misleading aiming, waist-level viewfinding, wide-angle framing,

CHOOSE YOUR VIEW

A high viewpoint narrows but slightly lengthens the nose, draws attention to the hair and forehead, and gives the face a triangular appearance. A low viewpoint tends to strengthen the chin, broadens but shortens the nose, and emphasises the eyes and brows - but beware of nostrils!

WANTED!

A void head-and-shoulders portraits with the subject turned to face the camera unless your intention is to create a passport snap or a 'wanted' poster. Instead, turn the subject so the picture captures a three-quarters perspective, narrowing the body. Tilt the head slightly so that the subject looks down the line of the shoulder into the picture. A pose like this will breathe life into a portrait and give it movement and interest.

or even a mirror turned at 45 degrees to the lens will get you the picture without the subject being aware. Misleading aiming involves your focusing at a point similar in distance to the subject. Hold the focus by retaining pressure on the shutter button, then turn to the subject and fire the shutter quickly before the victim is aware. Snap a second shot if your subject notices and decides to glare or confront you!

Candid Camera

With a preview LCD screen you can often frame and focus a picture away from eye height, enabling you to neatly conceal the fact that you're taking a photograph, or a small mirror held at 45 degrees to the lens will turn your pictures through a right angle - you'll be pointing ahead but photographing to the side. Setting the lens to its widest wide-angle setting will enable you to point the camera away - ostensibly - from

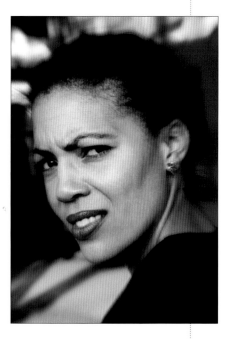

The classic head-and-shoulders pose with the subject's shoulder drawing the eye into the picture. Here, a longer focal length has blurred the background and flattened depth to really lift the subject out of the picture.

the subject you want to capture while actually including him or her in the picture.

Interaction between several subjects equates to interest in a picture. When working with a group of people, arrange them so that there is a variety of angles and heights - even if that means someone kneels. Avoid a straight line-up treatment which makes for dull, flat pictures. Couples make great subjects. Let them touch to heighten the human interest, which is the essence of what you're attempting to capture.

Arrange multiple subjects so that they're framed by something solid - tree trunks, steps or stairs, a doorway or a window. This will have the effect of joining and fixing the group in its own space, and provide a focus for the picture. Use your camera's wide-angle setting and exploit the ability of the lens to fill the frame.

Little and Large

It's a sure bet that most of the children you meet and photograph will be smaller than you. Yet time and again you'll see photographs of kids who all but disappear into a corner of the picture because the photographer is towering over them. The secret, if there is one, is to get down where the action is (unless you're trying to make a virtue of a child's relatively diminutive stature to give impact and poignancy to a picture). Allow your camera to see the world as children see it. Look for unusual child-eye view angles, use a fast shutter speed (if your digital camera lets you choose) and flash for action-stopping pics. Try shooting from a low viewpoint - that

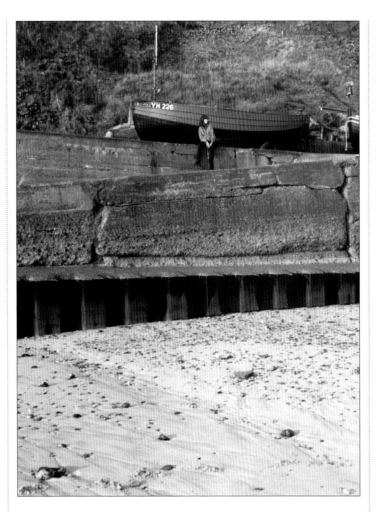

is one lower than that of the child subject, so you're looking up into the child's face, or exaggerate the height difference by standing close and photograph the child from almost directly overhead.

If you have kids, accompany them to a birthday party and take your camera with you. Better still, take them to the park on a sunny afternoon, let them run off to play with others, and wait for the picture to emerge.

Here again we can see the potential for drawing the eye into a picture. While the subject is but a tiny part of the overall image, there's interest in the 'layers' that arc horizontally across the scene, dividing it and heightening the visual impact and interest.

GETTING THE OUTSIDE IN

Step outside and you step into a world of possibilities, picture-wise. Landscapes are everywhere you look, even in cities, and buildings old and new are a joy to explore with a camera. And let's not forget the humble family seaside holiday – ice creams, donkey rides, and all!

From the moment you leave your home you're surrounded by landscapes that are potential pictures. A landscape can be the archetypal rolling countryside and scenes of farm buildings or a shot of distant office towers outlined against a dramatic sky.

If there's a secret to shooting landscapes, it is in rejecting the notion of including all that you can see into the picture in a bid to capture what you perceive as its breadth of scale. Instead, find a focal point that leads the eye into the scene and try to isolate a section of what you see. In a landscape, composition is vital, but by trying to incorporate the widest possible scene, you'll find that when the photograph is printed the lack of focal point results in a dull and empty picture. Try to avoid the obvious viewpoint. Raise yourself above the scene or get down low to tease out an interesting perspective.

The Light of Day

Time of day and the elements play a substantial part in the appearance of the landscape which is otherwise fixed. Patience will result in the picture you're looking for, and you may have to return to a subject when the light or the weather is better suited to the scene. Midday sun - the time when the sun

This picture *(left)* is a fascinating interplay of textures, light, shapes, reflections, and shadows. Look for contrasts like this in any landscape shot, and you'll have a stunning image.

By focusing and exposing for the scene outside, then standing back from the window, this picture *(right)* has a perfect frame. To achieve the same effect, stand close to the window and point your camera outside, squeezing the shutter release to enable the camera to focus on the scene and correctly determine a suitable exposure. Hold the shutter to 'lock' the settings, then take a step or two back and release the shutter. You may need to crop superfluous window material from the picture.

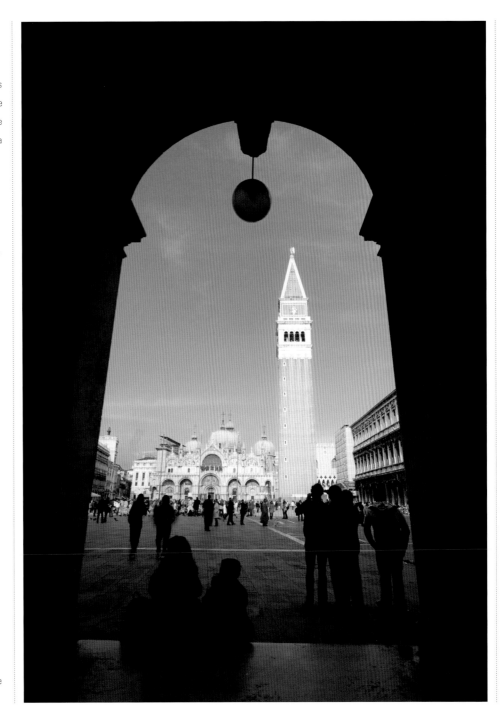

A delightful scene such as this *(left)* demands the rule of thirds for a balanced composition, but all the rules of exposure have been abandoned in order to capture the magnificent light.

is more or less directly overhead - results in few shadows and flat pictures. Morning and late afternoon sun casts deep shadows which reveal the texture in a scene and help you to build layers which draw the eye from the foreground to the background.

As you might expect, the seasons play an important part in the quality of light. During the summer months, your pictures will be well lit, but the light can be harsh, whereas in spring and autumn, the sun is lower in the sky, shadows are deeper and the natural world is alive with colour! Winter sunshine is thin and bright but beware of inaccurate exposure meter readings (and that includes automatic exposure digital cameras as well as those over which you

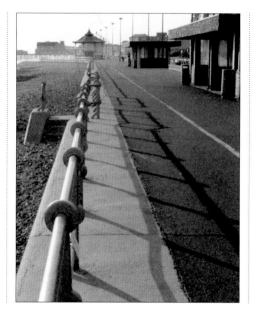

Any device that will draw the eye into the picture will create interest. Here though, the railing has become almost abstract and yet it's the main source of interest within the photograph.

The wintry trees in this scene *(below)* are almost abstract. What matters in the image are the colours and textures which strike a chord in the viewer.

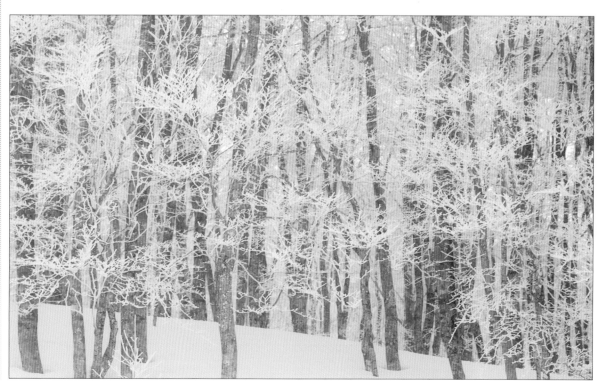

have control). Snow scenes especially can easily fool your camera into overexposing and it may be necessary to make EV and white balance adjustments accordingly.

Second only to weddings, holidays present ideal opportunities for taking pictures. Simple snaps of families gathered together on the beach, kids making sandcastles, donkey rides, and brightly coloured buckets and spades - pictures like these are perennial favourites. They evoke lovely memories of endless summer days and strike a chord that virtually everyone can relate to. No day at the beach is complete without your camera and far from being clichés, these classic shots will live as pictures long after your attempts at high art have stopped embarrassing you!

Edifying Edifices

Photographing buildings is in many ways like photographing any landscape; the difference lies in the combination of attraction with

purpose. All buildings have a function and a reason for their existence. Architects design buildings with a dominant aspect and by photographing this you capture the essence of what it is that makes the building interesting. Let your eye seek out the dominant features, and then move on to, and over, the supporting elements. A low viewpoint and a wide-angle lens setting will exaggerate these features and make for a very striking picture.

Opening the lens to its widest possible setting has resulted in wildly distorted angles in this picture of a windmill. However, the distortion emphasises the mill's sails and points the eye to the second windmill on the hill at the right of the image.

CLOSE QUARTERS

When photographing buildings, it's natural to imagine that the best pictures will include all or at least a substantial amount of the building in the picture by using a wide-angle lens or wide-angle setting zoom setting. But much of what good architecture is about is texture. Often getting up close and making an abstract of some small part of a building - worn bricks, scarred stonework, an old rusted lock, or similar - will capture the flavour of a building in a way that shooting it as a whole never could. See pages 62–65 for details of how to use your digital camera up close.

Point and Click

Buildings can be impressive in their own right, or because of the way they fit into or contrast with their surroundings. Those constructed on an impressive scale can be difficult to work into a picture in their entirety and you might have to think of alternative ways to shoot them. Look for a reflection in a store-window, a car's wing mirror, or even a puddle for a different perspective.

Scale and Elevation

Alternatively, photograph the building from afar, filling the frame as far as you are able with your camera's zooming function and cropping out unwanted material when the picture is downloaded to your image-editing software. Work your way around the building, taking pictures that reveal interesting nooks and crannies. Consider how light falls and is reflected against its elevations; study the space around the building; use street furniture and passers-by to provide a measure of scale. Now move in close and pick out the building's details, such

Don't overlook a simple picture-postcard scene such as this one *(above)*. Careful framing helps get all relevant detail into the image.

The distorted angles in this picture are what is known as 'converging verticals.' A wide-angled setting makes the building 'lean' backwards.

Although there's quite a bit of 'noise' in this night scene of lit buildings *(right)*, the artificial colours add emphasis to the hues from the buildings themselves and the whiff of steam from the centre building is the frosting on the cake! The Arc de Triomphe *(left)* appears a sea of calm and solidity among the bustling traffic in this long night exposure.

as doors and windows, steps and stairs, eaves, and the material of the building itself - bricks, stone, concrete, or whatever.

Landmarks are all very well, but it's the unfamiliar which makes an interesting picture when overseas. Street furniture such as road signs, electricity and telephone line poles, vending machines, post boxes and phone booths, quirky

Textures and colours again, but with a longer exposure they have created a softened tone for this image of pebbles on the shore.

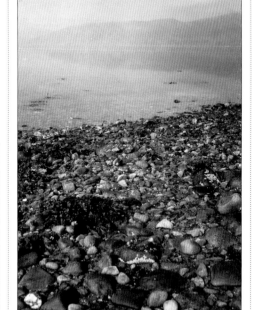

SAND IN THE MACHINE

In the course of regular use, a camera will come into contact with all kinds of potential contaminants, but none is quite as bad as sand. Fine grains will work their way into every thread and combine with the grease intended as a lubricant to form a grinding paste! It's possible to buy protective cases or you can save the clear plastic bags which wrap fruit, tying the bag tightly around the camera to keep out the sand.

A mixture of the natural and incongruous here makes for a splendid composition *(left)*. The fact that the brash yellow of the sign contrasts splendidly with the intense blue of the sky squeezes extra value from a great image.

(Right) An adjacent building to the Leaning Tower of Pisa has deliberately been included in this photograph to make a comparison and show just how much the tower actually leans!

delivery vehicles, public transport (trams especially), and street markets with exotic fruit all create a picture of things which are - literally - foreign to our experience.

All Abroad!

Of course, when in Paris, take pictures of the Eiffel Tower; in London, Tower Bridge, the Houses of Parliament, Nelson's column and Buckingham Palace; in San Francisco, the Golden Gate Bridge; and in New York, the Empire State Building and the Statue of Liberty. But don't dismiss the everyday stuff. Look into a potential scene and try to isolate what it is that makes it different from your

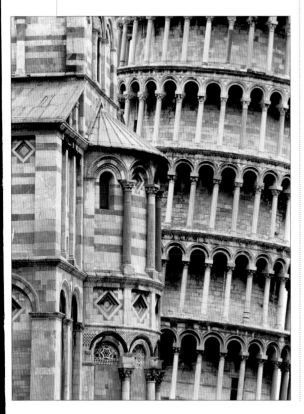

own home territory, and then take a picture that emphasises that difference.

Even the light itself can be different. If you live in a northerly clime and visit a region that's hotter, the light will be very different and will in some measure dictate the way that you approach pictures which might otherwise be familiar to you.

Like the photograph of pebbles on the opposite page, it is the soft tones and textures in this delightful picture of a rock pool *(above)* that make for a worthy photograph.

AN INSIDE JOB

With a new camera and an eye for subject matter, take a look around you. The home and garden offer interesting shapes, colours, and textures, and the potential for a peek into the daily lives of your family and friends...

It isn't only charity that begins at home. With a new digital camera fresh out of the box, your home becomes a veritable Aladdin's cave of picture-taking potential. Interiors, either 'straight' or viewed from unusual angles (from the foot of a stairwell, for example), create interesting photographs, and the possibilities for lighting effects are many and varied. Outdoors, the fabric of the building can also provide plenty of potential.

Arguably more important than all of these is that the home is the focus of everyday life - your life, and that of your family. And there are few photographs more compelling than the simple act of people, young and old, going about their daily routines.

These Four Walls

Taking pictures inside your home can be difficult. There are extremes of light and space. If the sun is shining brightly into a room, it's easy to fool your camera into making the wrong choice of exposure, and using flash often results in harsh shadows, colour casts, and red-eye if there are people in the shot.

Inside, try to look for ways to frame your pictures. By using, say, a doorway or a window to frame the subject, you'll strengthen the overall composition and create an illusion of

Even a subject as simple as a few dishes on a table can catch your eye and attract your lens. Wander through your home looking for interesting shapes and arrangements - especially when shot from an unusual angle.

WIDER THAN WIDE?

Most compact digital cameras sport a lens that is the equivalent of a 35mm SLR's 50mm lens. This has a field of vision that roughly matches the human eye. However, pointing a 50mm lens into an average room will cause much of it to appear outside the frame. If your camera has a wide-angle setting, use it to include more of the interior. Equivalent focal lengths would be 35mm (the largest focal length that is considered to be wide-angle) or 24mm (generally wide enough for most situations indoors). If your camera can swap lenses, plump for a 24mm or even a 20mm lens.

depth. It's important too, to ensure that the vertical surfaces in the room remain upright. Put the camera on a tripod and/or use its LCD preview screen if you find it difficult to keep everything upright using the viewfinder.

Placing people in a room will help provide a degree of scale, and if a person is seated, the room will appear to be larger. Position your subject midway across the room for the best effect. Take your picture from waist height; a shot taken at eye-level will include a lot of ceiling, and will unbalance the picture. Aiming the camera downwards will cause the walls to lean into the frame. Take your picture from a corner to get in the most detail, or point the camera through an open door.

Unless your camera is equipped with a wide-angle setting, it can be difficult to include much detail into a shot of a room. Try squeezing yourself into a corner and shoot from waist height to provide scale and balance.

UP CLOSE AND PERSONAL

Zoom in to the world of the microscopic and see things from a different viewpoint with close-up picture-taking. Most digital cameras offer close focus of some sort and there are add-on lenses for those that don't.

Taking close-ups is easy if your camera has a macro mode - and many do. Macro photography is what close-up picture-taking is properly called. In this context 'macro' is a focusing attribute which enables the lens to correctly focus an image inside the normal limit for its focal length. Sometimes this is achieved using an add-on macro lens, sometimes with on-board trickery, but whatever the method, close-ups enable you to take a 'sideways' look at a subject, exploring it in an interesting new way which might otherwise be missed.

Of course, it's entirely possible simply to download an 'ordinary' picture to your image-editing software, isolate a small section, and enlarge it, but the results would not be anywhere near as effective as a true close-up picture. The reason, as those who have read

Getting in close, without disturbing your subject, is only part of the secret of taking a picture like this one. This is where a good zoom or close-focus lens really comes into its own: not pulling distant objects into focus, but homing in on a near object and knocking its surroundings out of focus. The stunning effect is accentuated by the out-of-focus flower in the foreground. But when using autofocus, check carefully that the correct subject is sharp.

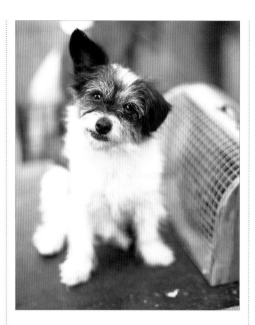

Using a powerful zoom or close-focus lens, a similar but equally striking effect to the butterfly image *(opposite)* can be achieved by knocking even some of the subject out of focus, and just focusing tightly in on the face or the eyes. This technique is useful for human portraits too.

HOW CLOSE IS CLOSE?

Close-up (or macro) lenses aren't measured in focal length in the same way normal lenses are. Instead a 'dioptre' rating is used. Dioptre is a measure of magnification and usually dioptre lenses are rated on a scale of between +1 and +10. +10 is used for really close-up work.

this book in sequence are by now aware, is that a digital image is constructed from pixels - a finite number of them. Enlarge a picture and you simply enlarge the pixels. Enlarge beyond a certain factor and the detail is lost - all that can be seen are pixels. In other words, there is no 'hidden' information in a digital image - what you see is what you get.

No Soft Solution

So, true close-ups are generated by your camera, not your software. And just how close you can get depends upon the make and model. A mid-range camera aimed at the hobbyist market will generally offer a close-up facility focusing between one and two feet. Some cameras adjust the flash output too so that a subject focused at such a critical range will be properly lit and exposed. Cheap cameras or older models may not have

a close-up facility (though even at this end of the camera spectrum most do) and those at the other end of the scale, some of the expensive 'pro' cameras, offer close-up photography at focusing distances of just a few inches.

One thing is certain, whether the distance is one foot or just one inch, if you're using

ADDING VALUE

If you want to get really close, you'll need to acquire add-on close-up lenses. Even if you're using a fixed-lens (not fixed-focus which is something else) compact camera - one which has a lens that can't be removed - you can probably buy and use one or more close-up lenses to suit. Many third-party accessories manufacturers offer lenses for digital cameras. Visit your camera manufacturer's web pages for details of add-ons, or use a search engine and search for something like 'lens+closeup+digital'. Close-focus lenses look very like magnifying glasses without a handle (because that's just what they are!) and as well as fitting to the camera they can be attached to each other to sum their dioptre values. That is, if you add a +10 and a +5 dioptre lens you'll get a +15-dioptre lens. Be aware that combining lenses in this way may result in some small degradation.

a point-and-shoot compact camera, what you see in the viewfinder will be far removed from what the lens is seeing. This phenomenon - known as 'parallax' - occurs because of the distance between the position of the viewing lens and the exposing lens. The few inches that separate these lenses on non-SLR cameras have little or no effect on framing when you're taking normal pictures, but draw near to the subject and the effect increases the closer you get.

Extreme Measures

Almost all compact cameras provide opaque framing guides (also known as correction, parallax, or close focus marks) visible in the viewfinder to help you frame at various distances. However, these might not assist in extreme close-ups. Instead, you must resort to the LCD preview screen to see what the lens is seeing and frame accurately (indeed, many cameras switch on the preview screen as soon as you enter close-up mode). Use the framing guides to position your subject within the viewfinder, so that the resulting picture shows the subject more or less where it should be.

Cameras with a 'macro' (close-up) feature let you get very close to a subject, but the 'depth of field' will not be great (the foreground and background will be out of focus).

The zoom feature won't let you get very close but the depth of field will be greater - although enlarging the picture to get the same subject will not yield the same detail as with a macro feature.

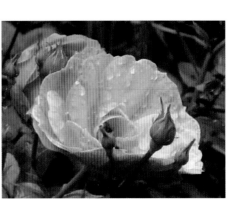

Nearest and Dearest

1 Good lighting and sharp focusing are essential for a quality close-up picture. Lighting can come from the camera's own flash or from external lamps, such as a couple of anglepoise lamps, though you should compensate for the tungsten bulb by using your camera's white balance function.

2 Mount the camera on a tripod. Switch on its close-up mode and position it so that the subject is framed in the way that you want. Position external lights if you're using them. Switch on the camera's timer function. This will enable an exposure to be made without inducing camera shake from the shutter button.

3 Squeeze the shutter release to lock focus, then fire the shutter. Move back so that your shadow doesn't obscure the subject, then stand still so that the camera isn't affected by vibration (which will appear in the picture as fuzzy focusing).

4 Sharpen the image once it's downloaded to your image editor using the techniques covered elsewhere in this book.

FIELD TRIP

When using a close-up lens, the depth of field will be reduced dramatically - possibly to as little as 15mm. This can have a significant impact on your picture. If you're shooting, say, a flower at close quarters, the depth of field may not even be sufficient to keep the whole flower in focus. You might find that while the petals on one side are pin-sharp, those on the other side are a complete blur. This can make for creative interest but it can also be simply irritating! To partly overcome the problem, use lots of light to enable you to use as small an aperture as possible. If you can, position your subject on a stiff sheet of white paper to throw light up and on to it. If you're shooting outdoors, in a meadow for example, you can use a piece of stiff white paper as a light deflector by locating it to the side and at an angle to the subject.

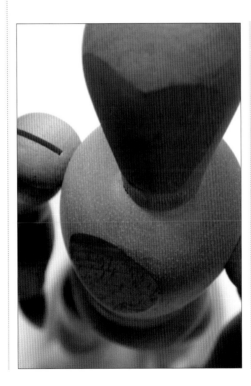

If you follow the steps outlined on this page carefully, you should achieve high-quality, close-up shots that give sharp detail and accurate colour.

HOW YOUR GARDEN GROWS

As the seasons shift and change, you'll have limitless possibilities for imaginative and stunning photographs. But each new season will present fresh challenges, as well as new blooms.

The garden is a great hunting ground for photographs. Obviously, the seasons will largely dictate what's of interest in any garden, but they also provide a shifting, ever-changing backdrop to your photographs. During the summer, there's fauna and flora in abundance, children playing on the grass, older family members dozing in chairs, and pets frolicking. Avoid the midday sun which casts few shadows (and results in flat, lifeless pictures), and shoot your photographs in the morning or late afternoon when the sun is at an angle in the sky and you can discover interesting nuances of light and shade.

Snowdrops and F-stops

During winter, and especially in the snow, the landscape of the garden is transformed dramatically. Snow reflects and boosts the available light. Your camera will expose incorrectly, and it's important to adjust using its EV (Exposure Value) function, which manually compensates for over- or under-exposure. Adjust by two EV stops to ensure that snow appears white; otherwise it will be captured as a mid-grey. Similarly, mist and fog require EV compensation of up to two stops to expose correctly and retain the white of the mist.

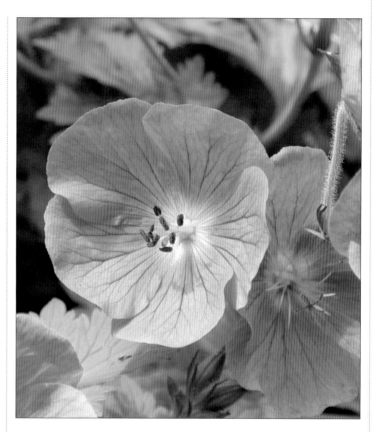

Using the macro feature on your camera lets you capture the splendid colours of nature *(above)* and in any image-editing software those colours can be further enhanced.

This photograph of a meadow *(right)* uses the brook to lead the eye to the focal point of the image.

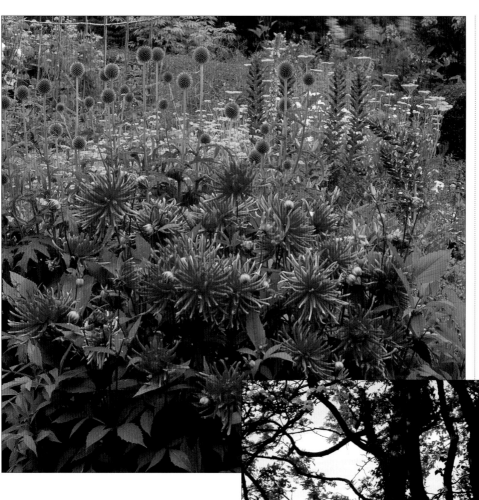

Keeping as low as possible to the level of borders of brightly coloured flowers *(left)* helps to bring out the amazing variety of colour, shape, and size of the plants.

The muted tones and interesting shapes of the branches and leaves of this tree *(right)* provide an enticing foreground to the country scene beyond.

White Out

Indoors, it's more than likely that you'll be shooting under artificial lights, which will mean either fluorescent striplights or conventional tungsten bulbs. Both will add an unwanted colour cast to your pictures, in this case reds or greens. Preview a shot with the on-board LCD and, if you find that it has a red or green cast, use your camera's white balance functions to compensate for the artificial lights. This function of your camera is also particularly useful in very white sunlight or in snowscapes. If your camera doesn't have a white balance option, you can simulate the effect using image-editing software once you have downloaded the images onto your computer.

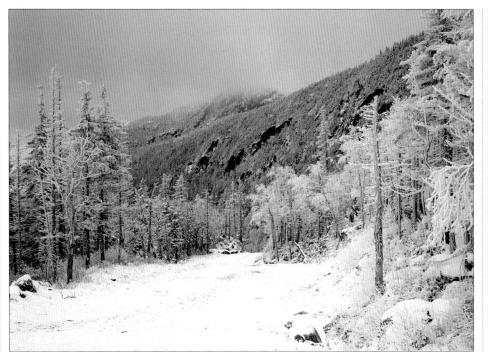

Shots of landscapes covered in a blanket of snow are often disappointingly grey *(above)* when you see the results. Most mid-range digital cameras feature white balance adjustment. This makes an allowance for the amount of white light, so that the image becomes less grey and the whites are purer *(left)*.

PETS AND OTHER ANIMALS

Animals provide great potential for photographers and those using a digital camera have an added advantage – there's no film to waste while taking the endless shots required to capture the 'right' picture! Start by practising with family pets and work your way up to bigger and wilder animals.

Everyone's heard the old thespian saying about 'never working with children and animals,' and there's a good reason for its passing into common usage (especially when applied to the latter category): animals are unpredictable! Even photographing loveable and friendly pets can be fraught with the unexpected problems. But photographing animals is fun and their behaviour can provide magical pictures - which is why actors dislike working with them so much, because no actor wants to be upstaged!

So haul out your digital camera, switch on the flash, and get to work around the house photographing your family pets. You know by now that, as a digital photographer, you have an automatic head start - you can shoot as many pictures as batteries will allow without wasting film, and continue until you get the picture you're after.

Good Behaviour

Start by watching the animal in question - say, a cat or a dog - and note the details of

Even a pet cat can be chivvied from his lair as a subject for a photograph! Invest time watching your pets in the home and garden so that you can determine their habits. Mount your camera on a tripod and settle yourself for a wait. When the picture comes along, you'll be prepared.

Dogs can make excellent subjects for photographs. Unlike humans, they're not aware of the camera and therefore don't exhibit any self-consciousness - they just strike a perfectly natural pose.

their behaviour, where and why they come and go. Both cats and dogs have favourite spots where they like to curl up for a nap. Cats generally prefer to raise themselves off the ground and choose somewhere warm, though many will also come and sit on a piece of paper for no apparent reason if you put a sheet down on the floor. Dogs (if they are allowed) enjoy sofas, beds, or a big cushion, a spot on the hearth before an open fire, or a stretch beneath a warm radiator.

Know Your Prey

Get to know their favourite places and you have a likely stalking ground for great pics. Choose your location, sit quietly with your camera, and wait for the picture to come into view. Wide-angle and zoom lenses work equally well for different reasons, and you can always crop to compensate for weak composition afterwards. The effort will be in capturing your pet at his most endearing, when he's displaying a human-like trait or action.

Caught in the Act

Many animals enjoy performing tricks. Cats like to catch small items that you throw for them, and will endlessly chase a bobbin or something similar attached to a length of string. Dogs are altogether easier creatures to train, and will happily sit down, roll over, hold out a paw, or balance a square of chocolate on their noses while you take a picture. Some dogs (especially the smaller breeds) will even do spectacular tricks like walking on hind legs.

The Right Way

Remember though that the secret of a great pet picture lies in encouraging your pet to do whatever catches his personality. Tricks are fun, but unless they say something about the pet, the potential for poignancy is lost. If you're trying to photograph small animals, fish, or reptiles - essentially those that are housed in glass or plastic tanks - beware of reflections from the tank, especially if you're using flash. A good idea is to set the camera on a tripod at a slight angle to the tank, and use the camera's timer to take the picture for you once you've checked for composition and focusing to avoid catching your own reflection. Also, a polarising filter will cut glare (hold it in front of the lens if your camera can't use filters).

There are super shots to be had outdoors too, but to find them you'll have to monitor

the animal's behaviour. Patience will reward you with the best picture, and your camera's zoom will get you closer to the action.

Open Forum

Zoos and animal parks are perfect starting points for larger animals. Photographers often struggle to shoot zoo pictures without including the cages in the shots. Digital photographers have no such problems. Using the photo editing techniques discussed later, it's possible to remove cage bars and other artificial obstructions, which would otherwise ruin a great photograph.

A photograph like this *(left)* is all about simply being in the right place at the right time - often entirely by accident. Be sure to carry your digital camera with you wherever you go with fresh batteries and free space on its memory card so you never miss a picture.

On the other hand, a trip to your local zoo or wildlife safari park will turn up lots of photographs like this *(below)*. The inmates are entirely used to having strange people point cameras at them! And of course with some deft image manipulation any annoying artificial artefacts *(left)* can easily be removed *(right)*.

But conventional techniques will work too, so position the camera as close to the cage as is practicable. Depth of field will ensure that it 'melts' into the shot. Use your camera's zoom lens function to enable you to span the safety barriers between you and the wilder inmates. A wide-angle setting is useful when photographing creatures indoors. And don't forget that the zoo is full of watchers as well as the watched and some of the visitors are every bit as rich a hunting ground as the inmates.

These geese have become almost abstract shapes within the picture, which makes it an intriguing composition.

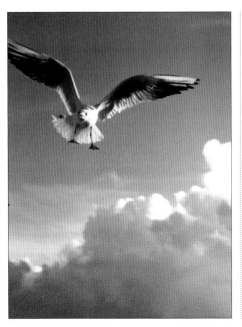

A fast shutter speed will stop action and enable you to capture birds in flight, though you might shoot many pictures before you get the 'right' one.

SPORTING CHANCE

The next time you go to watch a football match or cheer on your children at the school sports day, don't forget to take your digital camera. There's a wealth of picture-taking possibilities at every event.

Sporting events present fabulous opportunities for picture-taking. Indoors or out, solo, in teams, behind the wheel, mounted on horseback, with a bat and ball, a rod, or whatever, there are people, there is interaction, and moments of high drama followed by periods of extreme concentration - all grist to the photographer's mill.

You can approach sports pictures in two ways: if you're a fan of a particular sport, such as football, take along your camera whenever you set out to watch a match and log the game as it unfolds; alternatively, and for those who aren't great sports fans, think of sporting

If you've ever noticed professional photographers at a sports event, you'll have seen that they use very long lenses in order to get closer to the action. Many digital cameras offer a zoom of some description and though these are usually very modest compared with the professional models, they can help fill the frame and magnify the subject matter.

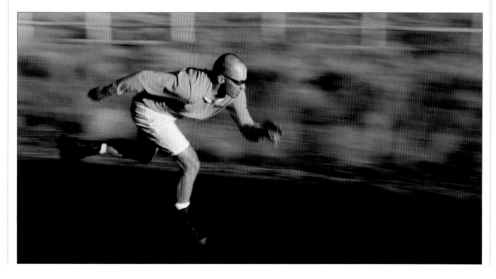

Panning a picture - moving the camera in time with the movement of the subject - heightens the impact and makes for a dynamic picture. The technique isn't difficult but requires practice. As a digital photographer you have a distinct advantage: you're not wasting film! If the results don't please you, discard them and take some more.

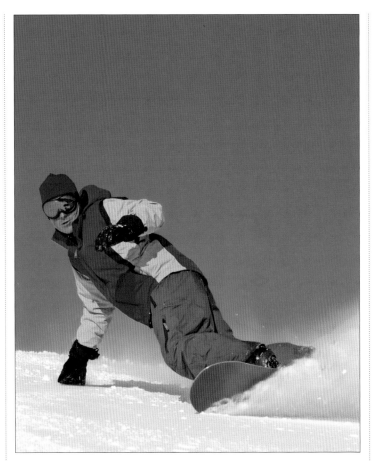

Mount the camera on a tripod, lock the focus on a point at which the subject(s) must pass through, and take a several pictures either one immediately after another or at intervals. The result is a striking action and time sequence, which truly conveys the atmosphere of the event.

events simply as opportunities for taking great pictures of people. In fact, it's almost certain that you've already taken pictures at sports events as a way to record the event for posterity - a school sports day, perhaps - but without really considering what you're doing as 'photography.' Now, you can combine the amazing features your digital camera provides with your burgeoning skills as a photographer to record these events for your family and friends while also taking pleasure in getting the best picture you can.

Unless you're photographing a chess match, in which case no one will be able to tell, a fast shutter speed will stop the action and capture some truly amazing pictures. This type of picture *(above)* is especially effective at events where capturing the natural grace of the body would otherwise be missed.

Using a slow shutter speed or moving the camera as you fire the shutter will result in a blurred picture *(above)*. However, this can be used to dramatic effect.

PLANES, TRAINS, AND AUTOMOBILES

We are surrounded by public and private transport of all kinds, some of which is attractive enough to warrant a picture! Your own vehicles, a vintage motorcycle perhaps, a steam train, or a yacht in full sail are all excellent subjects.

Endless pictures of a customised Ford, with gleaming paintwork and whitewall tyres, may bring back some memories for you, but they're very definitely best kept private! If you absolutely must take pictures of your motorised pride and joy, then now (i.e., putting into practice what you've learned in this book) is the time to do it with artistic aplomb. That way if the pics fall into the hands of those who might otherwise be entirely uninterested (your wife/children - and no apologies for assuming that it is the male who might be tempted!) they will have at least have some aesthetic merit.

In fact, pictures of cars, aeroplanes, steam trains, and all kinds of other weird and wonderful vehicles account for the bulk of professional photography sales around the world and, with care, you can ensure that transport pictures are interesting to look at for their own sake as well as, in future years, being a reminder of your youthful taste in cars!

Bring out the Best

The key to photographing inanimate and sometimes overfamiliar objects is to look at what makes them familiar, or attractive, and to find ways of accentuating those unique features. Try different viewpoints, such as close-up details of radiator grilles and badges, waist-high shots along the hood, or with a

Smile, please: the gorgeous curves and smiling radiator of this classic car are ideal subjects for the imaginative photographer. A flattering setting looks good in both, but the image on the left benefits from the viewpoint and use of a wide-angled lens to draw out the most prominent features.

gle detail - such as a headlight - in focus. ✓ using different lenses or settings: a wide-gle lens to distort the view from close up, a zoom to emphasise detail. A stunning ation helps: an English stately home would make a fitting setting for a vintage Jaguar or a Rolls-Royce, as would an urban setting for a classic sports car. And with the editing techniques we'll explore later, you could add some motion blur for extra dynamism!

LONG AND WIDE

The standard 50mm-equivalent lens is geared to everyday tasks, but lenses of longer and shorter focal lengths - or digital cameras sporting zoom lenses - are often better suited to particular tasks. So it is when taking pictures of vehicles. Interiors require the widest possible wide-angle settings to capture as much detail as possible. Exteriors also benefit immensely from a wide-angled lens setting which tends to exaggerate angles and can make an otherwise dull 'three-quarters' shot of our motor car (*opposite*), for example, look far more dynamic.

Long lenses too have their part to play. Zooming will fill the frame for a more dramatic picture and it will get you closer to the action - from an airport observation area or station platform, for example.

Boats make ideal pictures. With a little imagination and good composition their elegant curves and variety of textures

The Digital
Darkroom

Time was (and it was not so long ago) when photographers were required to carry around a heavy wooden camera on an unwieldy tripod, boxes of delicate glass plates, bottles of crude and sometimes dangerous chemicals, and a special tent that doubled up as a darkroom for developing 'in the field'. Fortunately Kodak's Box cameras ('You take the picture, we do the rest') simplified picture-taking, and the digital cameras of today continue that tradition, freeing your attention so that you can capture the picture you want without being overly concerned with the mechanics of exposing, developing, and printing. A desktop computer is your digital darkroom. You work in complete daylight, and enjoy instant results, but your mastery over the resulting images is absolute.

SOFTWARE

The digital darkroom is, in reality, image-editing software running on a computer. Your pictures are already 'developed' inside the camera, but download them to your computer, fire up your image-editing software, and your 'darkroom' is ready...

Until you print a picture from a digital camera, it exists as a digital file, just like a word processor or spreadsheet document. And, just like those other computer files, dedicated software is available to manipulate, edit, enhance, and print the file. All but the very cheapest cameras come with editing software for you to install on your computer. Sometimes this software will include the software for linking the camera and the computer to transfer the files; but it is rarely as sophisticated as third-party software.

Shop Smart

The leading image-editing software by far is Adobe Photoshop. Available for the Apple Macintosh and Windows PCs, Photoshop is a feature-packed program which, in experienced hands, can produce truly amazing results.

The disadvantages, however, are that many of Photoshop's features are confusing for novices, the interface is anything but intuitive, and the price is way beyond what the majority of home users might consider paying. Indeed, you can buy a good-quality, mid-range camera and editing software for what you'll pay for a copy of Photoshop. The program is absolutely without parallel in the marketplace, but unless you're a professional, or an amateur with a large bank balance, it might be better to look elsewhere.

Photoshop Elements' tool kit hides an amazing array of options beneath each of its buttons.

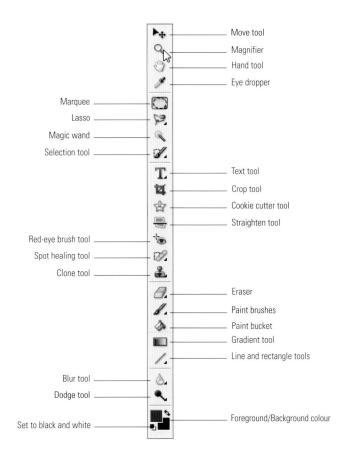

Move tool
Magnifier
Hand tool
Eye dropper

Marquee
Lasso
Magic wand
Selection tool

Text tool
Crop tool
Cookie cutter tool
Straighten tool

Red-eye brush tool
Spot healing tool
Clone tool

Eraser
Paint brushes
Paint bucket
Gradient tool
Line and rectangle tools

Blur tool
Dodge tool

Set to black and white
Foreground/Background colour

One alternative to Photoshop is Adobe's cut-down version, Photoshop Elements, which uses similar tools to its big brother, but at a vastly lower cost to the hobbyist.

It's Elementary

Targeted at the keen amateur, Photoshop Elements is geared to getting the most from digital camera images and among the tools and filters used to correct the kinds of problems you're likely to encounter are features such as colour correction, red-eye correction, merging backgrounds, constructing panoramas, straightening skewed pictures, and there's an integrated image browser too. The program also features a real-time compression option that enables you to squeeze the size of the file while viewing the effect on the image.

Pro Plus

For the PC only, one of the better-known programs – certainly the best value - is Paint Shop Pro, by Corel Software. Similar in many ways to Photoshop, Paint Shop Pro (PSP) offers a complete range of image-editing tools allied with an easy-to-use and intuitive interface. The program began life as a shareware offering, and you can still download, install, and run the latest version for 30 days before deciding to buy it. PSP is also often available on the CDs that accompany digital photography magazines.

The program features many dedicated digital photo tools including a scratch filter, red-eye removal tool, and auto contrast and colour balance enhancement. You can import pictures directly from your digital camera, and there's a built-in image browser.

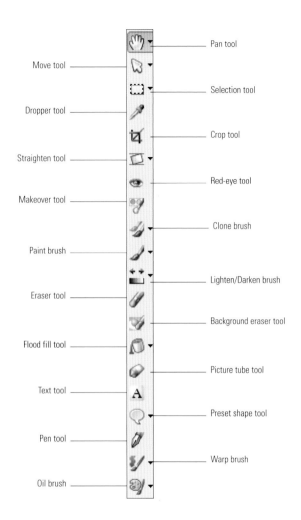

Move tool — Pan tool
— Selection tool
Dropper tool — Crop tool
Straighten tool —
— Red-eye tool
Makeover tool —
— Clone brush
Paint brush —
— Lighten/Darken brush
Eraser tool —
— Background eraser tool
Flood fill tool —
— Picture tube tool
Text tool —
— Preset shape tool
Pen tool —
— Warp brush
Oil brush —

And the Rest

If you have an Internet connection, try searching the Web for free downloads and shareware offerings. Many digital imaging and computer hobbyist magazines feature demo software on their cover-mounted CDs, too. Experiment until you find an image editor that suits you – when you do, you'll be amazed at the possibilities!

Paint Shop Pro has most of the tools the novice or semi-professional user will need. However, Mac users beware, this image-editing software is only available for PCs.

STEP 1 – SHARPEN & CONTRAST

It's time to open the door to your digital darkroom. Start with some simple editing – enhancing sharpness and adjusting contrast – and you'll soon be creating complex photomontage images, and exploring time-lapse picture-taking!

As you now know, digital images consist of many thousands of pixels and each one is individually addressable. What that equates to is the ability to edit at the pixel level - the most basic - and enjoy complete control over your images. If you were a skilled artist, you could actually 'paint' whole new features into your pictures a pixel at a time - people, buildings, whatever! For the rest of us, those with modest artistic ability, you can improve sharpness, enhance contrast, correct flaws in lighting and composition, tweak composition, edit out unsightly or unwanted 'features', crop for best effect, and much, much more using the tools provided by image-editing software.

Tools for the Job

A program such as Photoshop Elements or Corel's Paint Shop Pro provides incredible control over an image with comprehensive software toolboxes which pre-empt your requirements, and require little effort to get good results. So let's start by using Photoshop Elements on the PC, to sharpen and adjust the contrast of a typical digital photograph. You won't believe how easy it can be!

Sharpening

1 Fire up Elements by double-clicking its shortcut on the desktop or selecting it from the *Start* menu. When the welcome screen opens choose *Edit and Enhance Photos*. When Elements has opened a blank picture window press *Control + O (File > Open)* and navigate to the image you want to enhance, then click 'open'.

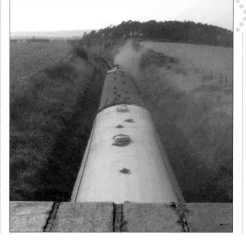

2 This picture of a train has the potential to become a very nice photograph. The wall creates a baseline from which the train leads the eye into the picture, and the tracks beyond continue the theme. The train bends slightly to the left, drawing the gaze into, rather than away from the image. But the nondescript sky and the slight fuzziness in some areas, together with late afternoon lighting, is spoiling the overall effect.

3 From the menu bar select *Enhance* then *Auto Sharpen*. The image is sharpened slightly.

4 At the *Enhance* menu again, select *Auto Sharpen* for a second time - the sharpening effect is dramatic. What happens if you apply the filter again? Try it. The image becomes almost pixelated. Press *Control + Z* once to undo the last edit (the second *Auto Sharpen*). Though the sharpened image appeals to the eye, the train is beginning to lose resolution, its once-smooth edges are now noticeably jagged. Fortunately, you can selectively sharpen an image. So let's start again.

5 Select *Revert* from the *Edit* menu to abandon all changes. Without selecting anything, apply *Auto Sharpen* to the entire image. Next, click on the *Freehand* lasso tool and draw around the wall to select it. Applying *Auto Sharpen* only to the wall throws it into relief, giving it an almost organic appearance. Even this simple two-step automatic sharpening has markedly improved the picture.

Contrast

1 The camera has captured smoke trails from the engine but the late afternoon sun has produced a hazy effect. Fortunately, this can be improved with a little contrast tweaking. Pull down the *Enhance* menu and select *Auto Contrast*. Elements automatically adjusts the contrast. Sometimes the automatic adjustment can be a bit crude so for a bit more control undo the auto contrast *(Control + Z)* and select *Enhance > Adjust Lighting > Brightness/Contrast*.

2 In the brightness/contrast window click the *Preview* button so it's ticked ('on') and experiment with the brightness and contrast slider bars. Your picture will change as you make adjustments and to see the 'before' image turn *Preview* off. Turn it on again to see the results of your adjustments. Click *OK* when you're happy with the way your picture looks.

3 If you decide you were too aggressive with your adjustments (which is easily done) press *Control + Z* to undo the adjustments. The secret is to experiment. Nothing is altered irrevocably until you save the picture. Now all that's needed is a bit of blue and some clouds in that sky. We'll get to that later!

STEP 2 – SELECTIVE FOCUSING

Almost all hobbyist digital cameras offer autofocusing as standard – you simply squeeze the shutter button and the camera does the rest – but it's surprising just how often the camera can be fooled. However, all is not lost with a poorly focused image if you have access to image-editing software.

While today's digital cameras are light and compact, and many feature complex systems to counterbalance external camera shake (i.e. caused by you as you hold the camera), it's still entirely possible to produce images that are not absolutely pin sharp. Earlier we looked at a simple method to improve the sharpness of your pictures, but there are many ways to counter the problem of poor focusing and we'll now look a little more closely at the tools on offer in image-editing software.

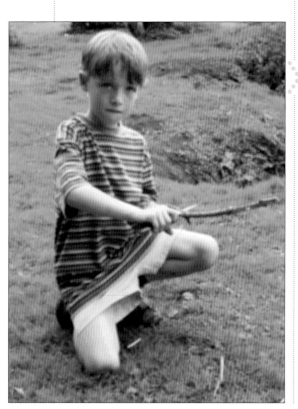

Hazy Routes

1 Along with the *Auto Sharpen* option, which merely increases the intensity of pixel tones where light and dark edges meet, most image-editing software features an *Unsharp Mask* (or something similar). This feature can work wonders with fuzzy, hazy images. Here we've opened the image in Elements.

2 Summon the *Unsharp Mask* dialogue box by pulling down the *Enhance* menu and selecting *Unsharp Mask*.

3 The enlarged preview window shows the 'after' effect of sharpening, and clicking and holding your mouse in the window will show the 'before' image. There are a number of settings on the dialogue that you can adjust (play with!), gauging the effect of each in the preview windows.

4 *Unsharp Mask* is a filter that increases further the intensity of contrast between mid- and high-contrast pixels. The *Radius* field specifies the number of pixels affected at an edge. *Amount* and *Threshold* denote the measure of intensity applied and the break-off point for pixels that are not affected by applying the filter.

5 Play with the controls until you become familiar with the effect each has on your image. Generally, a *Radius* of around 2, together with an *Amount* of 150 and *Threshold* set at 5 will give good overall results. The finished result should be an image like this *(above)*.

Further Clarification

1 Another excellent tool for enhancing sharpness is the *Clarify* tool provided by Paint Shop Pro. Open your fuzzy picture in PSP.

2 Pull down the *Adjust* menu and, from the *Brightness and Contrast* menu, select *Clarify*. Pictures are enhanced in a way that sometimes (depending upon the picture) even image-editing software experts would find hard to match using 'traditional' tools such as the *Unsharp Mask*.

3 Ensure *Preview On Image* is selected (to see the result of your changes on the background image) and either adjust the strength of the effect using the manual slider or numeric input box (from 1-20) or by selecting a preset value from the *Settings* drop-down tab.

4 *Clarify* will adjust the overall brightness and contrast of the image, which also gives the impression of extra sharpness. Used too heavily it can start to introduce artefacts though.

STEP 3 – CLEANING UP THE IMAGE

A vanishing act is easy when you manipulate your pictures with image-editing software. Remove noise, artefacts, and even undesirable features with the swish of a mouse and the click of a button...

Remarkably, digital images can be blighted (and sometimes enhanced!) by noise - not anything you can actually hear, but speckles in the picture caused by (among other things) low light levels. These appear as pixel-sized spots of colour throughout the image. Removing noise (or even adding it for effect - more of which later) is straight-forward, and many image-editing packages provide specific tools to do just that. It's a bit like deliberately generating a grainy photo-graph in conventional photography.

Stepped Edges

Artefacts occur in JPEG pictures which have been edited and saved many times. During every save the JPEG compression algorithm is applied, and eventually the picture begins to deteriorate and the edges of the subject matter appear become increasingly jagged - these are known as artefacts.

Speckled Image

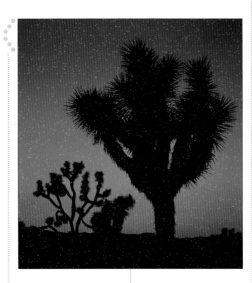

1 To remove noise speckles, open the troubled image (here in Photoshop Elements) then choose *Noise > Despeckle* from the *Filter* menu.

2 Elements will automatically remove detectable noise within the image. Some noisy images respond well to this algorithm, others poorly. If the latter holds true in your case, try this...

3 Access the *Filter* menu again and select *Noise > Reduce Noise*. A dialogue is displayed.

5 Sometimes, applying noise filters can have unexpected results (severe filtering can remove desirable information from a picture). Use *Control + Z* to undo the effect and try again using less smoothing until the balance is just right.

4 Use the sliders to increase or decrease the strength of the noise reduction according to the result in the preview window. Click *OK*.

BANISHING JAGGIES

1 Jaggies appear in digital pictures that have been overly compressed. JPEGs are especially vulnerable to this side-effect (known in JPEG parlance as 'artefacts'). To reduce JPEG artefacts using Photoshop Elements first open the image you want to correct.

2 Open *Filter > Noise > Reduce Noise*. At the bottom of the dialogue check the *JPEG Artefact Removal* box and make your adjustments.

3 Undo *(Control + Z)* will restore your image if the result is not to your liking.

Time for Change

1 The *Clone* (or *Rubber Stamp* in Elements) tool is ideal for removing unwanted features from an image, in this case an unsightly television aerial on the thatched roof of this cottage.

2 Open your picture and zoom in on the aerial. Don't get too close however; otherwise it becomes difficult to see how the cloning is blending in with the surrounding picture.

3 Select the *Clone Stamp* tool. Right-click (or shift click) an inch away from the aerial to specify a source for the *Clone* tool. Now move to your target, in this case the aerial, and press and hold the left mouse button. Crosshairs appear at the source point.

4 Move the *Clone* tool over the aerial so that it is covered by the material from the image picked up by the crosshairs. Continue until the aerial is 'removed'.

5 If it becomes obvious you've cloned from a specific area, try selecting a different source, clone, select again, and so on, to break up the result.

STEP 4 – ADJUSTING COLOUR

Our eyes are alive to the possibility of colour, and a lustrous, colour-saturated image captures a subject like nothing else can. Colours create mood, and colours imbue digital images with a reality that they might otherwise lack...

Unlike conventional photographs, the colour in digital images can be manipulated in order to tease the most from a picture. You can correct colour casts from artificial lighting and selectively increase colour saturation to add emphasis to a picture.

That's All, Folks

It's important to realise though, that making corrections to colour cannot add detail where none existed before. With a conventional negative, dodging and burning techniques (exposing more or less of sections of a print to the projected negative image) can uncover detail previously lost in shadow. A digital image has no secrets - what you see is what you get. The advantage is that each pixel can be changed to improve the image. The disadvantage is that unless you're skilled at drawing, you can't add features where none exists.

So improving colour starts with the camera and the exposure - use the features of your camera such as white balance and exposure compensation, review each picture taken immediately, and reshoot where possible. That way, you'll have the best possible exposure which can be enhanced further in the digital darkroom.

Saturate to Accumulate

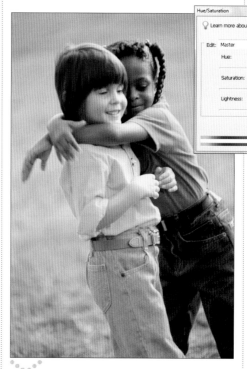

1 Contrast adds vitality to colours, but it's also possible to increase their intensity too much (just as you can turn up the colour on a TV). Open your image (here in Photoshop Elements), pull down the *Enhance* menu and, from the *Adjust Colour* submenu, select *Adjust Hue/Saturation (Control + U)*. The *Hue/Saturation* dialogue is displayed.

2 Ensure that *Master* is selected from the pop-up *Edit* menu at the top of the dialogue. Grab the *Saturation* slider and move slowly to the right to increase the colour intensity. Selecting *Master* means that the saturation of all the colours is increased.

3 You'll find that while some colours respond well to this adjustment, others such as skin tones don't. Access the *Edit* pop-up again and select *Reds*.

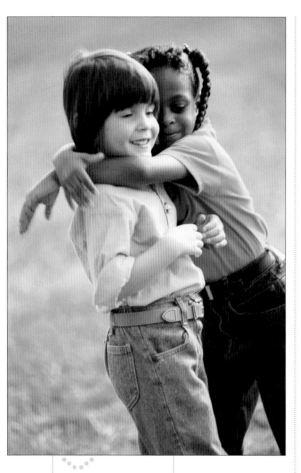

Add Life

1 Breathe life into flat, washed-out images by making simple adjustments to the contrast. It's an easy tweak in almost all image-editing software, and the first port of call to brighter colours.

2 Open the picture with an image editor (here Paint Shop Pro). Pull down the *Adjust* menu and select *Brightness/Contrast* from the *Brightness and Contrast* submenu *(Shift + B)*.

4 Use the *Saturation* slider to make skin tones more natural by moving to the left slightly. As you adjust, you'll see the picture itself change (if the dialogue's *Preview* checkbox is selected). Click *OK*.

5 As always, use *Control + Z* to undo changes and return to the *Adjust Hue/Saturation* dialogue to try again if you need to. Play with the colours until you begin to get a feel for balance. Remember - the image remains unchanged until you save!

3 Make small adjustments to contrast by typing a new figure into the *Contrast* field or click on the pop-up slider and move left or right to suit.

4 The preview windows on the dialogue box give a flavour of what to expect, but it's back at the image proper where you'll see the effect of the changes - make *Preview On Image* active to see the effect or use *Control + Z* to undo overly zealous adjustments and *Shift + B* to summon the adjustment dialogue for another go.

STEP 5 – ADJUSTING BRIGHTNESS

From simple overall brightness and contrast adjustments to the delicate tweaking of midtones, shadows, and highlights, image-editing software will enable you to save pictures that would otherwise be ruined by poor exposure...

How many pictures have you taken that were spoiled by being under- or over-exposed? Although it's possible to manipulate conventional negatives at the processing stage in order to lighten or darken them and improve contrast, and also to edit the resultant prints using dodging and burning techniques, the processes require that you do your own developing and printing. And that means a darkroom, enlarger, and lots of other expensive and unwieldy equipment!

All Change

Digital images, of course, are far easier to manip-ulate. Every pixel can be changed. They can be brightened, made darker, and changed in colour to suit your requirements and improve the resulting picture. In fact, improving exposure begins at the camera, where EV compensation and exposure locking (controls that enable you to alter the camera's exposure settings relative to its metered measurements) are a significant aid in correctly exposing a picture.

Comprehensive control, however, begins when the picture is opened in an image-editing program such as Photoshop Elements. Everything from simple changes in overall brightness and contrast to complex histogram-based adjustments are available.

Recovery

1 Because it's orientated towards digital photographs (rather than digital images that have been drawn or scanned), Photoshop Elements provides camera-like lighting tools and filters which echo those available in the real world.

2 Launch Photoshop Elements and open a poorly exposed image.

3 The first step is to darken the background slightly in order to strengthen detail. Pull down the *Enhance* menu and select *Adjust Lighting > Shadows/Highlights*. In the dialogue box set all the sliders to '0'.

4 Click on *Preview* to select it, and then use the *Darken Highlights* slider to make the sky a little darker. Then, use the *Lighten Shadows* slider to bring out all the detail in the shadow areas.

EV ADJUSTMENT

Before making an exposure, the metering system within a digital (or conventional) camera assesses available light and sets the aperture and shutter speed accordingly. This happens in a fraction of a second as you squeeze the shutter release button and, if there are subjects of strong contrast in the scene, the camera can easily be fooled into under-, or overexposing. To provide a degree of manual control, many digital cameras provide exposure compensation known as the EV control. By adjusting the EV control up or down, the camera can be made to increase (or decrease) the exposure by one stop (that is, from, say, 1/125th to 1/160th sec). Some cameras provide half-stop adjustments.

To use the EV control, take a picture in the usual way. Compensate for poor exposure by adjusting the EV control up or down and make another exposure. Review using your camera's LCD screen and adjust again as necessary.

Shadows/Highlights

Learn more about: Shadows/Highlights

OK
Cancel
☑ Preview

Lighten Shadows: 16 %

Darken Highlights: 20 %

Midtone Contrast: 50 %

5 The final step is to adjust the overall contrast, to balance the tonal range as darkening the highlights and lightening the shadows can make your pictures look a little bit 'flat'. Move the *Midtone Contrast* slider to the right to add contrast - but not too much!

6 With just a few simple adjustments, you should end up with a corrected image that looks something like this.

Gamma Correction

1 Adjusting the overall brightness and contrast of an image can work well - or result in the extremes of dark and light being bleached out. If this is the case, the result could be a washed-out and 'thin' picture.

2 The solution is to adjust the midtones (aka the 'gamma'), which are the portions of the picture that feature tones falling between the extremes. By singling out these tones, blacks remain black and whites white, while the intensity of everything else is increased.

3 Launch Paint Shop Pro and open an image you want to edit. Pressing *Shift + G* will call up the gamma correction dialogue.

4 Make sure the *Link* box is checked so that all the hues are affected equally, click and hold one of the sliders, and move it gradually to the right. As you do so, the preview window shows how the image is lightened. An adjustment of no more than about 1.1–1.5 should be enough to improve the picture. Click *OK*.

KEEPING STANDARDS

Gamma is a standard measure of the shift in contrast in an image, though it's usually used to refer to 'midtones'.

Levels

1 Full control over the tones in an image is provided by Photoshop Elements' *Levels* dialogue box. Summon the *Levels* by pulling down the *Enhance* menu and selecting *Adjust Lighting*, then *Levels* (*Adjust > Brightness and Contrast > Levels* in PaintShop Pro).

2 The first step is to examine the graph (or 'histogram' as it's known). If the majority of peaks fall to the left of the graph, the image is too dark and it needs to be lightened. If the majority fall to the right, the image is too light. If all the peaks are in the middle and there are few or none to the left and right, there aren't really any highlights and shadows, so the image probably lacks contrast.

3 Ensure the *Channels* pop-up menu (above the graph window) is showing *RGB*, then click and hold the highlights grab-handle (the rightmost triangle beneath the graph) and move it on the graph to where the histogram falls off. This whitens the white values in the image.

4 If there's a gap between the left edge of the graph window and the point at which the leftmost values begin to rise this means the deepest shadows are not truly black. Click and hold the shadows grab-handle (the leftmost triangle) and move it to the right, to the point where the histogram starts to rise.

5 To lighten or darken the images overall, use the *Midtone* grab-handle (the triangle in the middle). Move it to the right to darken an image, or to the left to lighten it.

6 You can also use the three *Eye-dropper* tools to automatically set your black and white points. Simply select the black eye-dropper and click on an area in the image that should be black or use the white dropper to identify a white area. The grey eye-dropper can be used to correct the colours – click on an area that should be grey and Elements will adjust everything else to match.

STEP 6 – COLOUR CASTS

Colour photography was once an expensive luxury. Today's digital cameras provide colour images that positively sing with vibrant, saturated colours – but they're not always entirely accurate.

Almost invariably, your camera will balance colour more than adequately and your snapshots are rendered in bright, beautiful colours that bring the pictures to life. But occasionally, and especially in adverse lighting conditions, the camera gets it wrong. If you were committing a picture to film, there'd be little that you could do to rescue it, but digital images lend themselves to extremes of manipulation, and image-editing software provides just the tools necessary for correcting inaccurate colour.

1 Colour casts occur principally when you shoot with flash under artificial lighting conditions. The light from tungsten bulbs can tint the picture with an overall yellowish or orangey hue. Similarly, fluorescent lights can give a green tinge to a picture. All good image-editing packages provide automatic colour balance controls to correct colour casts.

2 In Photoshop Elements you can use *Remove Colour Cast* from the *Enhance > Adjust Colour* menu. The tool is incredibly simple to use - you just click on an area of the image that should be white, grey or black and if there's a colour cast present, Elements removes it, correcting the whole image in the process. You can keep clicking on the image until you get it right.

Casting Colour

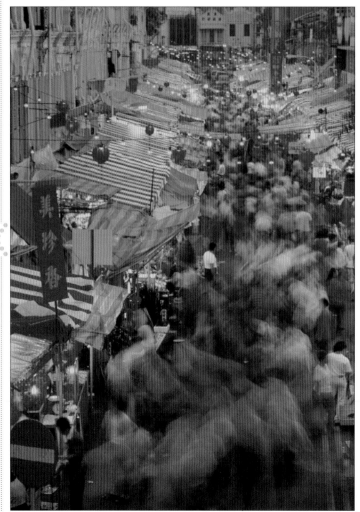

Variations on a Theme

1 If you want to take a little more control over your colour adjustments, then Photoshop Elements' *Variations* tool is also worth exploring. Select it by choosing *Enhance > Adjust Colour > Colour Variations* from the top menu bar.

2 The *Variations* dialogue is split into three main areas: before and after previews at the top; a series of eight thumbnails below; and a set of fine tuning options to the left. The thumbnails show you what the image will look like if you make that adjustment, and to make it simply click the thumbnail – the *After* preview is immediately changed accordingly to show the result.

3 To apply a colour adjustment to a specific part of the image you can click on the midtone, shadow or highlight buttons to the left – the default is midtones. This will let you adjust highlights and shadows independently. You can also use the saturation button to increase or decrease the intensity of the colour in your image.

4 You can click the thumbnails as many times as you like, adding or removing colours to build up the overall result. If you go wrong at any point, you can either click Reset Image or click on the Before preview to go back to square one. If you only want to go back one step, click on the thumbnail immediately above or below the one you last chose.

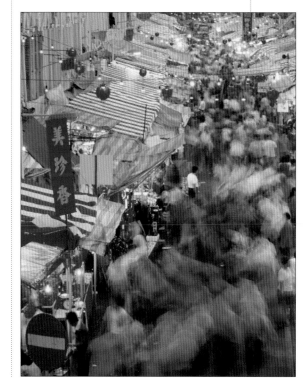

STEP 7 – ALTERING IMAGE SIZE

Conventional photographs are almost always enlargements of the original negatives. By using image-editing software digital photographs can be enlarged (or reduced) too, but just as in conventional photography, there's a small price to pay.

As you now know, digital images contain a finite number of pixels. Enlarge the image significantly and the pixel count must be increased - otherwise there'd be gaps where the original pixels were pulled apart.

Image-editing packages use a technique known as 'interpolation' to increase the pixel count. Sophisticated equations determine the properties of a new pixel based on those around it. Interpolation can be surprisingly accurate over small size increases, but larger increases soon lead to inconsistencies.

Small is Beautiful

But resizing images isn't always about making them bigger - often you'll want to reduce a picture. Images captured with multimegapixel cameras produce huge pictures - far larger than can be comfortably downloaded from the Web, for example. A multimegapixel image viewed on screen will be too big to see complete because digital pictures are reproduced pixel for pixel on a screen. For the most part, the Web is geared to work at screen resolutions of 800x600ppi (pixels per inch) and a big image will require sideways scrolling on the part of the recipient! But reducing the pixel count to a value of something less than 600ppi wide will enable the picture to be displayed comfortably.

Digital Enlarging

1 To see the current image size (and other information), click and hold the *Image Information* box in the lower left corner of the Photoshop Elements window or press *Shift + I* in PSP.

2 Resizing an image with either program is easy. In Photoshop Elements, pull down the *Image* menu and from the *Resize* submenu select *Image Size*.

3 You can resize the image by increasing its pixel count or by specifying a measurement in inches, centimetres, and so on – use the pop-up menus.

5 Check the *Resample Image* box, and choose a resampling. *Nearest Neighbor* is a fast algorithm but less accurate than *Bicubic*. However, it produces good results with subject matter that has hard edges. *Bicubic* is better for organic subjects. *Bilinear* falls somewhere between the two. Click *OK*.

4 Checking the *Constrain Proportions* box ensures that the photograph retains its correct aspect ratio (height to width), and that the image editor recalculates height or width based on your new figure for one or the other. The next thing to do is to resample the image by one of the options in the drop-down menu...

6 It's a good idea to *Save As (File > Save As,* or *Shift + Control + S)* so that you have the original to return to if you decide against the resized image.

Canvas Size

1 As well as resizing the image, you can resize the canvas by choosing *Image > Resize > Canvas Size* from the top menu.

2 Increase the canvas size of one image and copy and paste the other, cropping waste canvas when the images are aligned.

Reducing

1 Open your image with your chosen image-editing software.

2 From the *Resize* sub-menu under the *Image* menu, select *Image Size.*

3 Ensure the *Constrain Proportions* check box is crossed in the *Image Size* dialogue, and type 600 into the *Width* field in the *Pixel Dimensions* section of the dialogue.

4 Click *OK* and save the resized picture using *Save As* from the *File* menu. Not only will the physical dimensions of the image have been reduced, so will the file size.

Distorting

1 And this is what happens if you don't use the auto constrain function... scary!

2 The resized picture is distorted. *Control + Z* returns the image to its former size, and then start again with the *Image Size* dialogue. However, in some cases, distortion can add a desirable impact to a picture.

STEP 8 – SELECTIVE RETOUCHING

There are two areas in which photographs – conventional or digital – can go wrong: focus and exposure. We've looked at focus earlier in this chapter, so now let's turn our attention to the knotty problem of correcting poor exposures.

Correctly exposing a picture can be fraught with difficulties. Difficult lighting conditions, moving subjects, and automatic metering systems can all have an adverse effect on your pictures. Almost all modern cameras have built-in metering systems which work well, but scenes with strongly contrasting elements, overcast or very sunny days, night exposures, and artificial lighting can fool them into poorly exposing a picture. If you make regular use of your camera's LCD preview screen, this shouldn't be a problem - review the picture, and make another exposure using EV compensation and white balance controls to assist the metering.

Filling the Grey Areas

But let's assume you've made several exposures, none of which can be repeated and some of which have turned out to be poorly exposed: what can be done? A lot, in fact. Image-editing software can readily rescue pictures which might otherwise be discarded using built-in automatic tools, and those which can be customised to a particular image. Later in this chapter we'll look at correcting colour pictures, but first let's turn our attention to the greyscale image.

Dodge and Burn

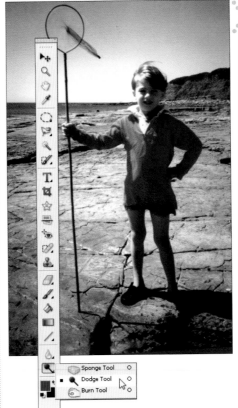

1 Photoshop Elements' *Dodge* and *Burn* tools make for excellent selective adjustments to small areas of an image. Both tools work equally well with greyscale and colour pictures, but they're especially useful when applied to black-and-white photographs, which can be tricky to enhance and balance when you're working with the overall image.

2 Select the *Dodge* tool from Photoshop Elements' *Tool* palette. *Dodge* and *Burn* sit with the *Sponge* tool, so if the *Dodge* tool isn't showing, right-click the sponge and choose the *Dodge* tool from the pop-up pick-list.

3 From the *Options* bar, choose a suitable brush from the pop-up palette – 65 works well for small areas, and 300 is excellent for balancing tone over larger areas. Select *Midtones* from the pop-up *Range* palette, and use the slider to enter a value of around 20% into the *Exposure* field.

4 Position the *Dodge* tool over the area you want to lighten, click and hold, then move the tool a little this way and that, until you begin to see the area brighten. Do this a little at a time (i.e. release the mouse button then click and hold again during the process) so that you can use *Control + Z* to go back a step if the dodging appears overly zealous.

STUCK IN THE MIDDLE?

Paint Shop Pro also offers dodge and burn tools to target and correct specific areas within an image, as well as a universal *Highlight/Midtone/Shadow* (HMS) adjustment tool. To use the HMS tool select it from the top menu *(Adjust > Brightness and Contrast > Highlight/Midtone/Shadow)*. Select *Relative Adjustment Method* from the bottom of the dialogue box and adjust the individual sliders to adjust each area respectively.

5 Experiment with the *Shadows* and *Highlights* settings too from the pop-up *Range* palette until the image is just right. *Save As* using the *File* menu or by pressing *Shift + Control + S*.

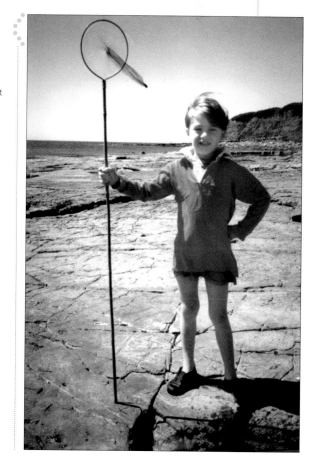

STEP 9 – CROPPING

Great pictures rely on strong compositions and creative cropping to emphasise the interesting elements within them. Cropping digital images is easy and fun, and forms the basis of all kinds of interesting special and novelty effects.

A major factor that sets professional pictures apart from those taken by novices is skilful cropping - trimming the unnecessary parts from a picture to draw attention to the area of interest. Indeed, there are few if any professional pictures - whether in galleries, newspapers, or magazines - which haven't been cropped. Even an already good picture can be made extra-special by a radical or adventurous crop.

Previously, of course, cropping was done at the darkroom stage. As the negative was projected onto photographic paper, the photographer zoomed in on the strongest element letting the rest spill over onto the enlarger's baseboard to be cropped out of the picture.

The Digital Way

Many digital cameras offer cropping facilities built in, and those which don't, of course, can transfer pictures to a computer for editing. But the good photographer should consider the composition first, and you'll learn over time to seek out the main areas of interest and compose the image in the frame.

Cropping in Paint Shop Pro

1 Some pictures demand to be cropped. Here, the interesting part of the picture is all too obvious — you just have to remove the useless material around it!

2 If you're using Paint Shop Pro, open the picture and select the *Crop* tool by clicking on it.

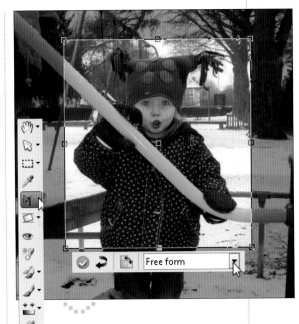

Free form

3 Move to the picture, click, and drag a rectangle around the part of the picture that you want to keep. When the rectangle encloses the desired part of the picture, release the mouse button.

Elemental Cropping

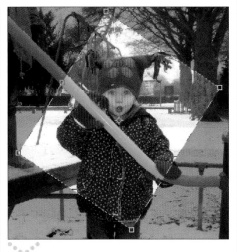

4 If you release the mouse button and find that the rectangle doesn't quite enclose the area you want, click and hold within the rectangle and relocate it. Alternatively, enlarge or reduce it by moving the mouse pointer over a side or corner. Click and drag to enlarge or reduce the image.

5 To perform the crop, click on the green tick below the crop box or double-click within the area of the rectangle. Press *Control + Z* to undo the crop and have another go.

1 Photoshop Elements offers a similar cropping solution in the form of the its own *Crop* tool...

2 Drag a rectangle (Adobe calls this a 'bounding box') around the picture selection you want to crop. Photoshop Elements displays the material which will be removed as an opaque 'shield'. This is useful in helping you to visualise how the cropped image will appear.

3 What's more, by moving your mouse outside the shielded area you can rotate the crop selection bounding box. At the lower right of the crop box are 'crop' and 'cancel' buttons. You can also double-click within the bounding box to crop.

4 You can switch off the crop shield by clicking the appropriate check box in the *Options* bar. If you'd prefer to view the shield as a colour, click the *Colour* box in the *Options* bar. Select a hue from the *Colour Picker* dialogue. To change the degree of opacity, use the *Opacity* slider or enter a value in the *Opacity* field on the *Options* bar.

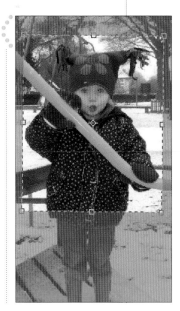

Just for Effect

1 Save your pictures from inducing sea-sickness in those who see them! Hand-in-hand with cropping, straightening an image which isn't quite on the level is easy using an image editor such as Photoshop Elements (shown here) or Paint Shop Pro.

2 Pull down the *Image* menu and, from the *Rotate* submenu, select either *Straighten and Crop Image* or *Straighten Image*. If the former would result in the image rotating outside of the window area (and thereby creating an irregular crop), enlarge the canvas (the imaginary area upon which the picture data sits).

3 Open the *Canvas Size* dialogue *(Image > Resize > Canvas Size)* and type new values into the *Width* and *Height* fields. Use the *Anchor* locater boxes to determine where the new canvas area will fall.

Super Vignettes

1 By combining cropped images (or crops of the same image in a new canvas) you can create interesting new effects such as this vignette-style image *(opposite)* with ease.

2 Open the picture and choose the *Elliptical Selection* tool (right-click the *Rectangular Selection* tool). Draw an ellipse around the picture and press *Control + C* to copy it to the clipboard.

If you're cropping to a particular size, for printing perhaps, or commercial processing, use a cropping mask – essentially, a blank picture of the required size into which you paste the picture, moving here and there and resizing until the material you don't want lies outside the mask. This is a good way of making sure images are ready to be printed to a specific size.

5 Click on the new canvas to select it and press *Control + V* again to paste in the new clipboard image as a selection. Move the image around to marry up the two to create the desired 'keyhole' effect...

3 Press *Control + N* and create a new canvas with an area large enough for experimenting (and based upon, say, three times the area of the original image). Press *Control + V* to paste the clipboard onto the canvas as a new selection.

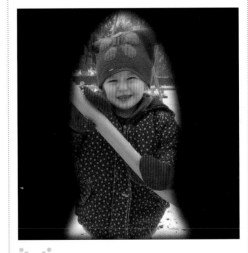

4 Back at the original, choose the *Freehand Lasso* tool to draw a new shape for cropping as shown here. Once again, press *Control + C* to copy the crop to the clipboard.

6 Select the *Crop* tool to draw around the 'keyhole', while leaving in enough of the black background to give the illusion of peeking through a keyhole!

5

Masterclass Tips

Image-editing software is to a darkroom what a 747 is to a Cessna: both will get you where you want to go, but there's a world of difference in range, speed, and comfort! Combine your digital camera with even entry-level editing software, and you'll have at your fingertips the kind of creative potential that photographers could only dream of previously. In the last chapter we covered a number of editing possibilities that demonstrated the type of tools and filters available to you, and we indulged in some fancy image manipulation. In this chapter - not for nothing entitled 'Masterclass Tips' - we'll continue that theme, exploring the more complex options and learning how to make what's in your mind's eye appear on your printer.

LESSON 1 – COMBINING IMAGES

Adjustments to your pictures – increasing contrast, tweaking colour saturation, and so on – are analogous to similar improvements within conventional photography but the ability to manipulate pixel-based pictures beyond the conventional makes for a world of possibilities.

All image-editing packages offer a range of what can only be described as 'special effects' - features for distorting, texturing, combining, and colouring images - and it's these that make digital photography such fun. Improving contrast or enhancing colour will make a good photograph from an otherwise ordinary one. Special-effects features - such as combining several pictures into one, mirroring, distorting, adding grain, feathering for highlighting and shadows, or the really wild special effects such as transforming your pin-sharp digital image into something resembling a watercolour or an impressionist painting - can really stretch your imagination to the the limit!

Don't Overdo It

It's fair to say that many of the more outrageous special effects can become tiring, and it's often difficult to see where you might use some of them (but kids love playing with special effects!). However, it's when manipulating pictures that might otherwise be discarded that digital photography and image-editing software come into their own. And even as a beginner, you'll find that creating amazing effects is easy with a bit of practice.

Make Do and Mend

1 Here's an example of the kind of manipulation that makes image-editing software such a powerful tool - even for beginners. This picture of rolling fields of hay is spoiled by a nondescript grey sky. A fix is just a click, a cut, and a paste away...

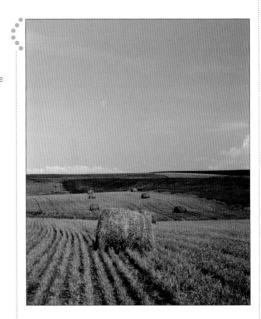

2 Launch your image editor and open the picture you want to correct. Select another picture that features an attractive sky. Using the *Marquee* tool, draw around a selection of sky and press *Control + C* to copy it to the clipboard.

3 Open the original image and paste the recently copied sky onto it. Here we've used Photoshop Elements and have called this Layer 1.

4 Now make just the original image layer visible and active. Using the *Magic Wand* tool, with appropriate tolerance (95 is used here) select just the sky area.

5 Next make the new sky layer visible and active. Invert the selected area and delete. The new sky now follows the horizon line of the fields and your new composite image is complete.

6 The finished picture. There's much more that can be done, but with even just a simple cut and paste from another picture we've improved this one enormously. As you work through the more advanced examples, you'll begin to see the possibilities for manipulating your own pictures and developing your skills along the way.

LESSON 2 – DISTORTING IMAGES

Distortion techniques have long been used by professional photographers to heighten the impact of a picture. The ability to distort digital images easily opens an incredible palette of creative effects that will enable you to go far beyond the simple family snapshot.

Anyone familiar with the music of the Beatles will be aware of the photograph of the band used on the cover of the 'Rubber Soul' album. The photographer produced a distorted, rubbery image by projecting a transparency of the image at an angle and reshooting it. The effect was and is startling: eye-catching certainly, but with an underlying tension that is at once unsettling and compelling.

If you've experimented with wide-angle lenses or a wide-angle setting on your digital camera's zoom lens, you'll have noticed that features become exaggerated or diminished depending on where the camera is in relation to the subject, and shooting tall buildings causes them to 'lean' in relation to each other (the effect is known as 'converging verticals').

Don't Look Now

Whether caused by the lens or manipulation of the picture once it's transferred to the computer, distortion can have a dramatic effect - even slight distortion is in some way unsettling because it makes us look at the world in a way that is different from reality. However, as with all visual effects, remember this works better on some photographs than on others.

In a Spin

1 Photoshop Elements is particularly well endowed with distortion filters (more are available as third-party plug-ins), and some of them are truly spectacular!

2 Try this: open a picture in Photoshop Elements - one that features a tall subject will work especially well.

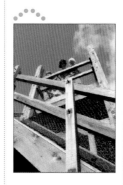

3 Pull down the *Filter* menu and select *Polar Coordinates* from the *Distort* submenu. When the *Polar Coordinates* dialogue is displayed click the *Rectangular to Polar* button then click *OK*.

4 Now soften the edges of the join. Select the *Blur* tool from the tool palette. Pop up the *Brush* menu on the *Options* bar, and select Brush 46 (or a similarly loosely defined brush). Set the *Brush Strength* value to 60%. Click and rub the *Blur* tool over the sharply defined edges of the image.

5 All that remains is to crop the background that no longer contains picture data, and then save the results.

Hall of Mirrors

1 Open an image (a group portrait works well) in Photoshop Elements. Summon the *Shear* dialogue *(Filter > Distort > Shear)*. Click and move the line in the distort grid at the top left of the dialogue. The image is distorted along the curves you specify. Make sure *Repeat Edge Pixels* is active.

2 Using the *Pinch* distortion filter *(Filter > Distort > Pinch)* you can distort an image so that its centre is 'pushed' or 'pulled' towards the viewer.

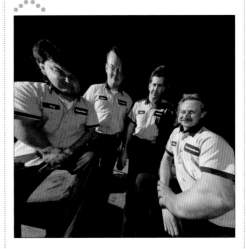

3 Get the fish-eye lens effect with the *Spherize* filter *(Filter > Distort > Spherize)*. Use the slider to determine whether distortion will be concave or convex, vertical, horizontal, or spherical. Crop the image to further emphasise the effect.

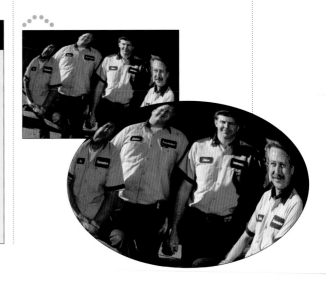

DISTORTION DOCTOR

Distortion is an eye-catching effect, but there may be occasions when you'd prefer to go the other way: to straighten an image that has unintentional distortion generated by the camera's lens. Andromeda Software offers a Photoshop plug-in to do just that. LensDoc is an easy-to-use utility for image-editing software that can make use of Photoshop plug-ins. A demo is available for download at *www.andromeda.com.*

LESSON 3 – ADDING TEXTURE

Not content with the visual impact of your pictures? Spice them up by adding a sprinkling of texture. Known as 'noise', it is the equivalent of creating a grainy conventional picture. It's very atmospheric, particularly with black-and-white images.

Previously we examined the issue of digital noise - speckles of colour that invade, and can blight, an otherwise attractive picture by appearing randomly throughout. These speckles can be removed quite easily using the ready-made tools provided by most image-editing packages. We tried one or two of them, such as the *Reduce Noise* and *Despeckle* tools in Photoshop Elements in the previous chapter, and there are others which we'll look at elsewhere on these pages. Those packages that don't sport noise-reduction filters can be used manually to remove noise (but the task can be onerous).

Not All Noise Annoys

Paradoxically, you might actually want to add noise! Contrary to normal intuition, inserting speckles where none existed previously isn't necessarily a quick route to a spoiled picture. A noisy image can simply be a grainy one which, given the right subject matter and tonal value - a gritty black-and-white street scene, perhaps - is enhanced by the 'realism' that noise brings. First though, let's look at one or two further options for removing noise.

Gritbusters 1

1 Although more usually associated with colour images, noise can affect black-and-white pictures too. Elements provides several tools that work with both colour and black-and-white pictures, but especially well with the latter. Launch Elements and open your image.

2 Pull down the *Filter* menu and, from the *Noise* submenu, select the *Median* filter. Although it is intended for use on small selections that are markedly different from the overall picture, the *Median* filter also works well when applied to an entire image if you use it sparingly.

3 The strength of the *Median* filter runs from 1-100, but over an entire image a high value will produce a 'soft focus' effect and lose a lot of detail. The rule is to use as little as possible to remove the noise, but not fine detail.

4 Experiment with a value of about 3 pixels and click *OK*. Much of the grain is removed and a little of the fine detail, but apply the *Unsharp Mask* and your image will be crisp again.

Median

| OK |
| Cancel |
☑ Preview

－ 25% ＋

Radius: 3 pixels

Adding Texture

Gritbusters 2

1 Paint Shop Pro's *Salt and Pepper* filter *(Adjust > Add/Remove Noise > Salt and Pepper)* works especially well with greyscale images. By determining when a light or dark speckle in a picture differs substantially from its neighbours, the speckle can be removed.

2 Fine detail is easily lost using *Salt and Pepper*, so select smaller areas of the picture without fine detail and apply the filter. Experiment with the speck size and sensitivity sliders until you balance the removal of speckles with the loss of detail.

3 Afterwards, use the *Sharpen More* and *Clarify* filters to add contrast and sharpness to the overall image. But don't overuse the *Sharpen More* filter.

4 Unlike the *Salt and Pepper* and *Median* filters, *Texture Preserving Smooth (Adjust > Add/Remove Noise)* attempts to retain detail while ridding an image of speckles. It does this by working selectively.

5 Once again, experiment by entering different values into the *Amount of correction* field and gauging the trade-off between retaining detail and losing noise.

True Grit

1 Adding noise to an image - particularly a black-and-white picture - can give it a 'period' feel. A street scene perhaps, or a train station will respond well to a greyscale and grain treatment as shown here in Photoshop.

2 There's no need to start with a black-and-white picture. If the image you want to manipulate is in colour, begin by discarding the colour data. Here the picture was changed using *Enhance > Adjust Colour > Remove Colour.*

3 From the *Filter* menu, select *Noise > Add Noise.* You can experiment with the amount of noise - 10 is a good starting point. Click the *Uniform* button and make sure *Monochrome* is checked.

4 What was at first a pretty, but dull picture of a main street is transformed into a period piece that harks back to a bygone era.

LESSON 4 – MOTION EFFECTS

You don't always want your pictures to appear razor-sharp. Add a bit of dynamism by using creative blurring techniques (and especially adapted filters) to give the illusion of motion to your pictures.

Earlier, we looked at correcting out-of-focus, fuzzy images - the result of camera movement, low light, or a moving subject - by applying various software filters, but there are times, strangely, when you might actually want to blur an image rather than sharpen it. Creative use of blurring can be used to give an impression of speed and a degree of 'movement' to your pictures - a shot of a moving car or motorcycle, for example. Photographers using conventional equipment pan the camera - that is, move it in time with the moving subject - while using a slowish shutter speed.

Panning

Panning has the effect of keeping the subject in focus while blurring the background, thereby recreating the sense of speedy movement. Digital photographers can pan by moving their cameras too, but it isn't an easy technique to master. However, there's another way to get more or less the same effect which is fun and requires little effort!

Panning Motion

1 Conventional panning is easy to try, but difficult to master, so let's cheat to get the same effect using image-editing software. First open your preferred software - here Photoshop Elements - then load a suitable picture, in this case, a BMX cyclist.

2 Carefully draw around the cyclist with the *Freehand Lasso* tool, then copy it to the clipboard by pulling down the *Edit* menu and selecting *Copy (Control + C)*.

3 Right-click on the image to deselect the selection. Pull down the *Filter* menu and, from the *Blur* submenu, select *Motion Blur*. The *Motion Blur* dialogue is displayed.

4 Click and hold the *Direction* pointer and rotate it to the opposite direction to that of the bicycle (so that if it is travelling to the left, rotate the pointer to the right). Now move the *Intensity* slider so that a figure of about 10 pixels is shown. Don't apply too much blur – it's easy to lose all definition! Click *OK*.

6 It may be necessary to soften - 'feather' - the edges of the cyclist slightly to get him to sit comfortably within the picture again. Using the *Freehand Lasso* tool, make a selection a few pixels in from the edge of the cyclist, and select *Feathering* from the *Selections* dialogue. A figure of about 20 pixels should be enough to aid blending.

5 Back at the now blurred picture, press *Control + V* to paste the copied image of the cyclist back into the picture as a selection. Take care to position it exactly over the existing, but blurred cyclist – instant panning!

7 The finished picture replicates remarkably accurately the effect achieved when panning in a more conventional way. The cyclist is frozen in action, while the spectators in the background are blurred, giving the impression of camera movement.

LESSON 5 – VIGNETTES

Have fun transforming your nearest and dearest into living antiques using sepia tones, and some creative cropping and feathering techniques. These make up an instant ageing process that is fun to try and attractive to display to others.

Many cameras provide a range of effects that can be applied before the images even leave the camera for the relative safety of your computer. A perennial favourite is sepia toning, which makes an instant antique of virtually any photograph. The technique is best applied to portraits and is especially good when combined with other effects such as 'feathering' - cropping and softening the edges of a picture - from within an image editor.

If your camera provides sepia toning 'at source' then by all means apply it and save yourself the trouble when the picture is imported into the image software (though it might be that toning from the software provides a better result, so experiment).

If the camera doesn't offer the effect, follow the steps outlined here to create living antiques of your friends and relatives - they'll be delighted!

Eight Steps to Tone

1 Select a suitable image. While almost any picture can be artfully cropped and sepia-toned, a portrait works best - head and shoulders or full length with one or more subjects.

2 Launch your favourite image-editing software (here Photoshop Elements) and open the picture.

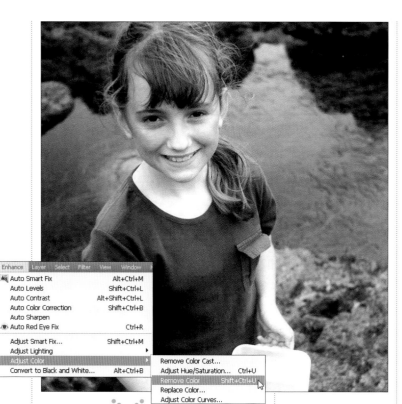

6 Press *Shift + Control + I* to select the background and pull down the *Select* menu and choose *Feather*. Feather the selection by around 50 pixels , press *OK* and then press *Delete* - the background is removed leaving the subject with a soft feathered edge.

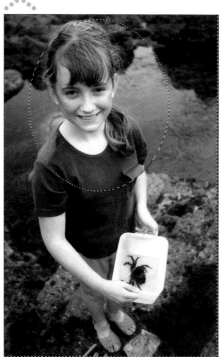

3 Begin by discarding existing colour information. Pull down the *Enhance* menu and, from the *Adjust Colour* submenu, select *Remove Colour* (or press *Shift + Control + U*). The picture is rendered in black-and-white.

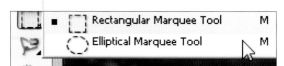

4 Artful cropping enhances the ultimate 'aged' effect. Select the *Elliptical Marquee* tool by clicking on it. The tool defaults to the *Rectangular Marquee* tool. If yours is rectangular, right click on it and choose the *Elliptical* tool.

5 Draw an ellipse over the image by clicking, holding, and dragging. If it isn't positioned quite right you can click on it and move it until it's just right once you've drawn the ellipse,

7 Apply the sepia tone by selecting *Filter > Adjustments > Photo Filter*. In the *Photo Filter* dialogue, select *Sepia* from the drop-down filter menu. To adjust the intensity of the tone slide the density slider to the right - in this instance 90% gave a nicely toned image.

8 The finished result, looking for all the world like it came from a Kodak No.1 camera, circa 1900!

LESSON 6 – ADDING EFFECTS

Many image-editing programs provide a number of interesting and fun texture effects to apply to your pictures. Some of the texture filters are extremely effective while others are, well, clichéd at best. But all are fun to play with and, used sparingly, can enhance an otherwise dull picture.

Texture effects really come into their own when used to create greetings cards, T-shirts, and the like - a novelty finish is just the thing to grab the attention! How best to use the texture and similar special effects? Experiment! *Control + Z* will undo any effect, or you can simply abandon the picture without saving or *Save As* to make a copy. Only by playing with the effects provided by your image-editing software will you envisage what can be done and where best each can be applied. Only a few pictures lend themselves to this kind of treatment, but the results when they do can be startling!

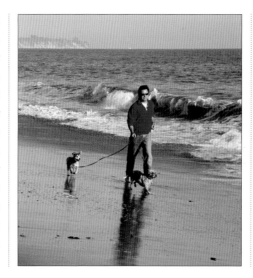

The same image again, but this time after having PSP's *Coloured Chalk* effect applied *(Effects > Art Media Effects > Coloured Chalk).*

Paint Shop Pro's *Black Pencil* effect *(Effects > Art Media Effects > Black Pencil)* adds a kind of stippling effect to this greyscale picture, transforming it into a sketchpad drawing.

Instant artist! PSP's *Brush Strokes* effect transforms a digital picture into a work of - traditional - art. Experiment with the length and density of the strokes, the width, opacity, and number of bristles in the 'paint brush'.

Photoshop Elements' *Liquify* filter *(Filter > Distort > Liquify)* can be used to create all kinds of interesting effects. Set the *Brush* size to a low value, say, 10, and you can tinker gently with straight edges in a picture to soften them. A large brush of, say, 130, combined with a pressure of about 15 or 20, will completely transform an image!

Instant artist! Elements' *Watercolour* filter *(Filter > Artistic > Watercolour)* gives a painterly finish to any digital picture.

Ocean Ripple (Filter > Distort > Ocean Ripple) makes an image appear as if it's being viewed through a piece of frosted glass. Colour pictures respond exceptionally well to this effect. The distinction between colours is blurred, but their intensity is enhanced. Elements also provides a distortion filter called *Glass (Filter > Distort > Glass)* which has a similar, but more intense result.

Extrude is a very popular effect that can be seen in advertisements, magazines, and flyers. Photoshop Elements makes recreating the effect easy. Open your picture, pull down the *Filter* menu, and select *Extrude* from the *Stylize* submenu.

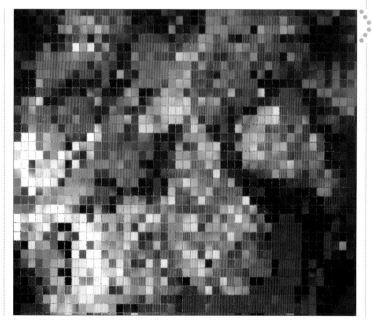

This *Mosaic* effect in Photoshop Elements *(Filter > Pixelate > Mosaic)* is marvellous for creating 'robot vision' (think kids' birthday cards). Use it with brightly coloured abstract images for a vista of hues.

And here's yet another way to recreate the illusion of motion within a static image. The *Wind* filter *(Filter > Stylize > Wind)* slides pixels left or right to give the effect of a strong gust of wind! You choose between *Wind*, *Blast,* or *Stagger*!

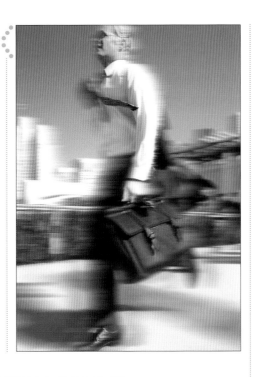

IN EFFECT...

Photoshop Elements' *Texturizer* function offers a range of effects, but you can expand on these by acquiring third-party 'plug-in' effects packages.

1 Use your favourite Web search engine to locate plug-in Photoshop Texture effects. Try searching on 'Photoshop' and 'texture' (in this way: +photoshop+texture or 'photoshop texture').

2 Select from those on offer and download them to your computer.

3 From the *Texturizer* dialogue, access the pop-up *Texture* menu and select the *Load Texture* option. Navigate to the downloaded textures using the file browser.

4 Apply the new textures by choosing them from the pop-up *Texture* menu in the usual way.

Or for the ultimate in textured canvas effects, summon Elements' *Texturizer* dialogue *(Filter> Texture> Texturizer)* and select from brick, burlap, sandstone, and so on. Use the *Scaling* and *Relief* sliders to determine the size and depth of texture.

LESSON 7 – CREATING PANORAMAS

See the world in 360 degrees using photomontage techniques – this impressive effect combines lots of individual pictures into a single uninterrupted image that spans an entire horizon.

In the 1950s and 60s a number of imported cameras became available which would take a panoramic photograph spanning more or less everything from left to everything right in front of the photographer. These were used quite seriously to capture images of large groups of subjects such as parades of soldiers, engines, and carriages - even wedding pictures! The panoramic camera featured a swivelling slitted lens housing which turned through 180 degrees. The slit admitted light a slice at a time to reach and expose the film within.

By Hand

Many photographers copied the technique using ordinary cameras. By standing in one spot, taking a picture, turning to the left or right slightly, taking another picture and so on, the resulting prints can be cut up and stitched together to make one long photograph.

As a digital photographer you have the means to produce truly incredible panoramas and photomontages. Some cameras actually enable you to create a composite image at source using software within the camera itself. But even if yours doesn't stitch together images, using editing software is easy. Some image editors (notably Photoshop Elements) provide specialist tools for panoramic shots.

Stitch Up

1 Let's assume your camera doesn't provide panoramic shooting, and your image-editing software is of the plain-vanilla type. The first step is to take the pictures that will become the panorama. This is best done with the aid of a tripod or other steady rest to ensure that all the images are taken at the same height (though even then corrections can be made digitally). Allow plenty of overlap between each image and try to keep the same distance from the subject to preserve the perspective over what will become the composite panorama. Launch your software and browse the images.

2 Select what will be the first in the sequence and open it (here with PSP). Ensure the picture is selected and press *Shift + I* to summon the image information dialogue. Make a note of the picture's dimensions. Repeat for each image that will be featured in the montage.

3 Press *Control + N* and create a new picture box based on the collective dimensions of the pictures for the montage. Give yourself plenty of elbow room - you can crop neatly when the images are in place.

4 With the first image in the sequence open on screen, press *Control + A* to select the entire picture. Copy it to the clipboard by pressing *Control + C* and then click on your new blank document to select it.

5 Select the empty picture box and press *Control + L* to paste the first image into the new picture window as a layer. Repeat the select/copy/ process routine for each image in your panorama.

6 As each image has been pasted in as an individual layer, you can move them independently to align them using the *Move* tool. You can also adjust each one's colour, brightness and contrast so they match one another for added consistency.

7 Although the new image is complete, the joins are hardly seamless! Select the *Clone* tool, right-click a 'clone source' and disguise the join between the pictures. Crop the image, flatten the layers and save.

Painless Panoramas

1 If your image-editing software provides the necessary tools to stitch together separate images, the task will be easier still! Here is Photoshop Elements.

2 As before, ensure your sequence is taken on a tripod, in light that is not subject to wild changes (i.e. a nice, blue sky and no clouds to create unwanted shadows). Maintain perspective where possible by staying at a uniform distance from the chosen subject.

3 Open the *Photomerge* dialogue from the *File > New* menu and click the *Browse* button. Navigate to the folder that contains your images. *Shift-click* over the range of pictures and click *Open*.

4 Elements now takes over, opening, positioning and adapting the sequence of pictures to make a single image. Sit back and watch the fireworks!

5 Elements' *Photomerge* will make an excellent attempt at automatically merging the images into one panoramic picture, or you can choose to position them manually before the program smoothes away the edges.

6 When the composite is created, the *Photomerge* screen is displayed. The *Preview* window shows the image as it will look before cropping. Use the *Navigator* window to move around the preview image by clicking and moving the red rectangle.

7 Click *Advanced Blending* in *Composition Settings* to flatten and blend the image and click *Preview* to see a preview of the effects. Click *Exit Preview* when you've viewed it and click OK when you're ready to create your panorama.

8 Back in the Elements editing window, use the *Crop* tool to remove unwanted areas from the image (such as the overlaps above and below), and use levels and colour adjustments to finish off the picture.

9 All that remains is to save the panoramic image using *Save* or *Save As* from the *File* menu.

LESSON 8 – CREATING SOFT FOCUS

A blurred image isn't necessarily a bad one if the blurring is used selectively to create a 'softer' atmosphere. The technique is used by photographers all the time and it's one that lends itself perfectly to being replicated in the digital darkroom!

The old saying that 'the camera never lies' is only partly true. Certainly what the camera's lens sees is what the camera captures on film or digital storage card, but there are many tricks and techniques which can ensure that what the end-viewer sees is something markedly different to what was snapped. Of course, these techniques are not intended in any way to fool those who see the picture - they're used to enhance it.

Premeditated or Not

To achieve a soft-focus effect, conventional photographers use various filters fitted to their lenses which help to diffuse the light and create a softer, slightly misty atmosphere without throwing the subject out of focus. To achieve this effect the conventional photographer must decide in advance whether or not to use a soft focus filter. Not so the digital photographer; with basic image-editing software the same effect can be achieved in a matter of moments, and applied to any image that is suitable.

Sharp and Sweet

1 Only after taking this picture did it become clear that the subject's light colouring would lend itself well to a soft-focus effect. It really is easy to achieve.

MOVING TARGET

Soft focus and blurring can also be used effectively to create the illusion of movement. One way to achieve this is known as panning - a technique which can also be synthesised in the digital darkroom. Turn to pages 112–113 for details of how to do it.

2 Open the image with your image-editing software (here Photoshop Elements was used). Duplicate the image either via the *Layers* menu, or by dragging the existing image onto the *New Layer* icon as shown here.

FIELD STUDIES

Depth of field (aka 'depth of focus') is the portion of a picture between the foreground and furthest point at which the image is in focus. Lenses of different focal lengths offer different depths of field. Combined with aperture, it's easy to isolate a focal point. That's why a moderately long lens of, say, 85mm to 135mm is ideal for portraiture. The depth of field is compressed, flattening features and enabling a strong focal point to enhance the subject.

3 Select the duplicated layer (called *Background Copy*) and apply an small amount of the *Gaussian Blur* filter *(Filter > Blur > Gaussian Blur).*

4 The next step is to set the background copy's blending mode to *Lighten* (accessed via the *Layers* menu). This will allow the original background layer to show through.

5 Finally, position the background copy layer over the original layer. The blurred, but slightly opaque copy will create a diffuse effect similar to using a conventional soft-focus filter over your camera's lens.

LESSON 9 – ALTERING BACKDROPS

*Build incredible pictures by combining separate images – one on top of the other – in a
kind of layered sandwich, editing each until they appear exactly how you want them,
and then merging for a final effect that can't be equalled using a single image.*

Working with layers is the great secret of master image manipulators and the frosting on the cake of the best image-editing software such as Adobe Photoshop, Photoshop Elements, and Corel's Paint Shop Pro.

That power lies in the ability layers give you to construct a composite image by combining pictures, one on top the other, each of which can be edited individually without in any way affecting the other layers. In this way it's possible to enhance everyday pictures beyond measure, and create fantastic special effects and convincing montages and panoramas.

Mix and Match

You can rotate layers, colour, and render them transparent, link one or more together to apply an effect across several layers, and import and delete them. Image editors that support layers generally provide a palette of some sort so you can see at a glance the layers that make up an image along with their attributes. When you're satisfied that the picture is how you want it, you can compress all the layers into one to reduce the size of the file, but without compromising quality. So now let's explore a fun example of using layers.

Spirit of Fun

1 There are many famous - but faked - photographs of people in incongruous settings. But whereas in the 'good old days' of conventional photography, photographers had to go to painstaking lengths to achieve barely believable results, in the wonderful world of digital imaging, it is now possible to travel just about anywhere in the world. You, your family, and your friends could be sunning themselves in the Caribbean in next to no time. It's easy to source some holiday destinations - spend just two minutes on the Web and you'll find you have countless, albeit low-res, exotic paradises to choose from.

2 Select a suitable image of the people that you want to send on a dream holiday of a lifetime.

3 Using the *Freehand Lasso* tool, carefully draw around the figures. It is worth spending time doing this, as the more accurately you draw around them the more realistic the effect. Select *Copy* from the *Edit* menu (Command + C).

4 Select the image you want to use as your background and press *Control + V* to paste the selection as a new layer. You can switch between the two layers in the *Layers Palette*, which can be found under *Window > Layers*.

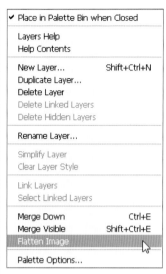

At any time you can select and reposition the top layer by clicking on it and using the *Move* tool. Drag the image to move it or use the arrow keys to nudge it into place. When the picture appears as you want it, flatten the layers in the image by selecting *Flatten* from the *Layers* menu and *Save As* from the *File* menu.

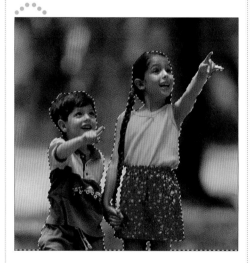

5 By clicking on each layer in turn you can use the various image-editing tools to ensure the tones and colours of the new image and the background are balanced.

LESSON 10 – ADDING WORDS

A picture, so the old saying goes, is worth a thousand words, and while it's certainly true, there are times, believe it or not, when a line or two of text can make all the difference to your pictures.

By now you're probably tiring of us extolling the virtues of the digital over the conventional. It's true that photographs from film are often of higher quality (in terms of resolution and colour rendition) than their digitised counterparts and that digital photography is still relatively expensive, even considering the lack of processing. But digital photography is so supremely flexible and the pictures accessible - no darkroom, no chemicals, and complete mastery over the images, as you know so well by now. And one more truly useful advantage in the digital world is the ability to add text to your pictures, and not just plain text either!

Say it in Words

Combining text and images presents some marvellous opportunities to create greetings cards, flyers and handbills for club events, church fairs and so on, documents in support of your business or simply to enhance the image and give it a new twist!

There are many ways to add words, such as a simple line of text that is a caption to the picture, as a separate and fancy greeting or slogan, or as part of the picture itself, the letters embossed or stencil-cut from the subject matter of the image.

Words and Pictures

1 At its simplest level, adding a line of text to a picture is easy using image-editing software, though it's rarely possible simply to type text on top of the picture as you do when you enter text into a word-processor document. Instead, position a cursor on the picture, summon a text dialogue, and enter the text into that cursor position afterward. Photoshop Elements is one of the few packages that enables you to type text into pictures as effortlessly as if you were typing in a word processor. First, launch Photoshop Elements and open the selected picture.

Toronto at night

2 Select the *Horizontal Type* tool in the *Tool* palette. Click on the picture where you want the words and type your text.

3 You can select the font, size, and colour using the menus and fields in the *Options* bar.

5 Move the cursor around the edges of the text until it changes to this text-moving pointer. Click and hold, and you can position the text exactly where you want it.

4 The *Warp Text* dialogue from the *Options* bar provides a range of ready-made text shaping algorithms that you can apply simply by selecting one from the pop-up *Style* menu and using the slider bars in the dialogue to determine the level of the selected effect.

6 The end result. You can apply the same technique to any picture you like. It's deal for party invitations, parties and so on.

Warp Text

Style: None

None
Arc
Arc Lower
Arc Upper

Arch
Bulge
Shell Lower
Shell Upper

Flag
Wave
Fish
Rise

Fisheye
Inflate
Squeeze
Twist

OK
Cancel

Bend: %
Horizont   %
Vertical   %

Toronto at night

Shadow World

1 A drop shadow is a darker version of the text which sits behind and slightly to one side of the foreground text, making the background type, in effect, a shadow. Drop shadows can be seen everywhere in newspapers and magazines and they look particularly good when applied to photographs. Fortunately, they're also easy to make!

2 Launch your chosen image editor (here Photoshop Elements) and open a suitable picture.

3 Click on the *Horizontal Type* tool to select it. Choose a font and size from the drop-down menus on the *Options* bar.

4 Click to position the cursor where you want to type the text (you can move it later) and start typing. Use the text moving pointer to locate the text exactly where you want it.

7 To create a soft drop shadow effect choose the *Gaussian Blur* filter *(Filter > Blur > Gaussian Blur)* and apply a radius of around 10 pixels. The optimum blur amount will depend on the size of your text to start with.

5 Next, duplicate your text layer and select the lower layer in the *Layers* palette. Using the *Nudge tool* and the arrow keys move the lower layer to the right and down slightly.

8 You can now adjust the colour of the drop shadow by using the *Hue/Saturation* control. With the *Colorize* option checked adjust the sliders to change the text colour.

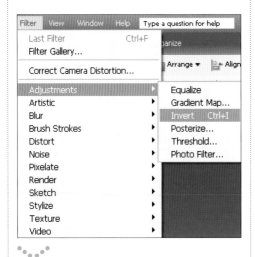

6 Choose *More > Simplify* from the Layers palette to convert the text to a raster image. You can now choose *Filter > Adjustments > Invert* to change the underlying text colour.

LESSON 11 – FRAMING

Surround your shots with an attractive border and you'll strengthen the contents within. Some cameras provide built-in border functions, and you can create and apply them in image-editing software too...

The popularity of borders - the edges which frame a picture - waxes and wanes according to changes in taste. Once, all photographs sported a white border a few millimetres wide. The border is actually an unexposed area of the photographic paper on which the print is created. In the 1970s, the vogue for borderless prints was all-pervading. Today, both are available but borderless prints are probably slightly more popular than the bordered variety.

What's often missed in the bid for greater image area is that far from taking something away from a picture, a border can strengthen the composition and provide a reference point against which the picture is balanced.

Many digital cameras offer a number of frames that you can apply to a picture before it's downloaded to your computer, and of course, adding all kinds of plain and fancy frames is easy once your picture has been opened within image-editing software.

Bordering Beauty

If the borders provided with your image-editing software, don't fit the bill, Extensis PhotoFrame, a third-party plug-in, has plenty on offer.

1 Photoshop Elements and many other image editors offer picture-framing functions. Start by launching your software and open a picture.

2 Open the *Artwork and Effects* palette from the *Window* option on the menu bar.

ON-BOARD BORDER

If your camera offers a selection of built-in frames, you usually apply them by selecting one before taking the picture. Flick through the frames on offer, choose one, and size and position it using the LCD preview screen, then take your picture. Often it's possible to download more frames to your camera from third-party suppliers or even design and download your own. Refer to your camera's directions for details. The disadvantage of using built-in frames is that they become part of your picture - you can only remove them by cropping using image-editing software.

3 Select the top left frame icon (the frame and sun icon) and choose *Frames* from the first drop-down menu. Select the frame type from the second drop-down tab to see a range of frame styles.

4 When you've chosen your frame click *Apply*. A box appears around your image and the slider at the top allows you to scale the picture to suit the frame. When you're happy, click the *tick* icon to apply the frame to your picture.

5 Click *OK* and the border is applied. Press *Control + Z* if you decide the border isn't right for the picture.

LESSON 12 – COLOURING

Colour photography has long been available and all digital cameras take saturated images that are nothing short of lavish in their rendition of colours. Yet hand-colouring a black-and-white image can make for a striking picture, and the process is easy using image-editing software.

There are two kinds of hand colouring. The first involves your taking a black-and-white photograph and adding artificial colour. The other type of colouring might better be described as hand 'uncolouring' and we'll show you that technique over the page.

A hand-coloured photograph has an aesthetic - and perhaps even artistic - value beyond that of the picture alone.

The mechanics of colouring are made exponentially easier using a computer and a digital image, but getting good results continues to be a fine art (in every sense)

though much of the fun lies in the execution. You can colour old black-and-white photographs you've copied with your digital camera or grabbed with a scanner, greyscale digital pictures you've taken yourself, or even a colour picture from which you've discarded the colour information!

Decolourising - taking the colour out of an image leaving only a small coloured portion - is easier, but it can add a great deal of impact to a picture. The effect is often used on advertising billboards, precisely because it is so eye-catching.

Adding

1 Select a picture you want to hand colour and open it with your chosen image-editing software (here Photoshop Elements). Remove the colour information using *Enhance > Adjust Colour > Remove Colour.*

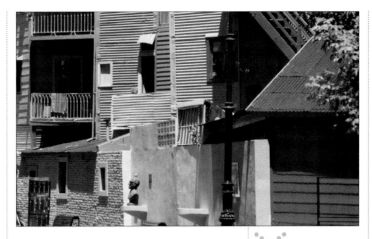

2 We're going to apply the hand colouring to a new layer, so open the *Layers* palette and click on the *New Layer* icon. At the top of the layers palette change the layer's blending mode from *Normal* to *Colour*.

3 Select the *Paintbrush* tool and on the options bar change the opacity to 50%. Double-click on the *Colour Chooser* to open the colour and pick a suitable colour for the area you want to paint.

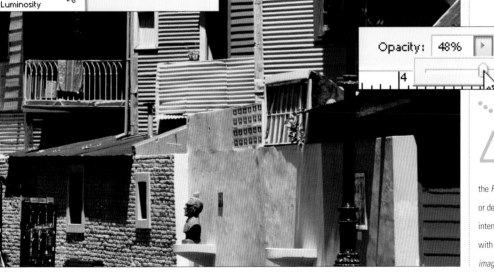

4 You can now paint onto the image. Change the opacity of the *Paintbrush* tool to increase or decrease the colour intensity. When you're happy with the result, click *Flatten image* in the *Layers Palette*.

Subtracting

1 Decolourising an image (i.e. discarding all colour information except one part of the picture) can be done in several ways. Those who've read through Chapter 5 and now know how to manipulate layers can work with two copies of the same image, one greyscale, one colour, throwing away all but the small colour element in one, and flattening the two layers so that they merge into a decolourised image. However, there are far easier ways to get more or less the same effect. Try this...

2 Launch your image editor (here Photoshop Elements) and open the picture you want to decolourise.

3 Select the *Lasso* tool, and carefully draw around what will be the colour subject in the image. Press *Shift + Control + I* to select the background.

4 Pull down the *Enhance* menu and select *Remove Colour* from the *Adjust Colour* submenu (or press *Shift + Control + U*). The colour information is discarded from the picture.

Auto Smart Fix	Alt+Ctrl+M	
Auto Levels	Shift+Ctrl+L	
Auto Contrast	Alt+Shift+Ctrl+L	
Auto Color Correction	Shift+Ctrl+B	
Auto Sharpen		
Auto Red Eye Fix	Ctrl+R	
Adjust Smart Fix...	Shift+Ctrl+M	
Adjust Lighting	▶	
Adjust Color	▶	Remove Color Cast...
Convert to Black and White...	Alt+Ctrl+B	Adjust Hue/Saturation... Ctrl+
		Remove Color Shift+Ctrl+
Unsharp Mask...		Replace Color...
Adjust Sharpness...		Adjust Color Curves...
		Adjust Color for Skin Tone...
		Defringe Layer...
		Color Variations...

5 Use the *Clone Stamp* tool to decolourise small areas missed when you have selected the subject with the *Lasso* tool. Next select *Save As* from the *File* menu.

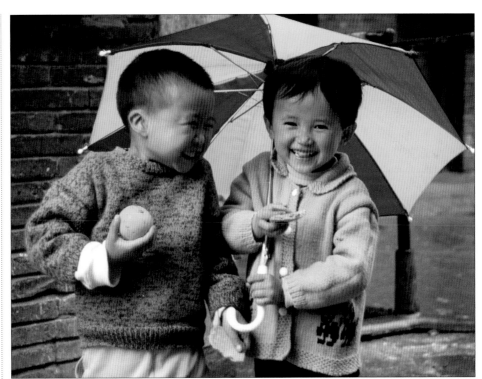

LESSON 13 – AIRBRUSHING

It's time to bring it all together and put yourself in the picture using the techniques discussed in this and earlier chapters. If you've ever wanted to stand shoulder to shoulder with Laurel and Hardy or be the fifth Beatle, now's your chance.

Woody Allen and Steve Martin have both starred in movies that featured shots of them spliced with clips of long-dead politicians, gangsters, celebrities, and film stars; even some beer commercials got in on the act. *Zelig* and *Dead Men Don't Wear Plaid* explore the amazing possibilities of using clever camera and editing trickery to fit Allen and Martin into clips filmed years earlier, some from Hollywood, others sourced from newsreels of real-life events. If you have seen either film (but particularly *Zelig*) you'll know how amazing the results can be.

Join the Stars

Now it's your turn. With your digital camera, image-editing software, and the techniques we've worked through elsewhere in this book, cutting in on the action is relatively easy and great fun! Amaze your family and friends and rub shoulders with stars of the past and present. Here's how…

Rewrite History

1 First catch your celebrity! You can use a picture of a politician, actor, sports star, notorious criminal - even a character from history. A picture that features the celebrity alongside another person is best as you can simply substitute yourself for the companion! A word of warning, however, be careful not to infringe any copyright laws if you intend to put your picture up for public consumption.

2 Using the print copying methods discussed later, digitise the celebrity picture. A scanner is best for this task but if you don't have one, you can use your digital camera and get reasonable results (see pages 148–149).

4 Download the picture and open it in your image editor. Next, open and activate the picture of the celebrity. Select *Image Size* from the *Image* menu and make a note of the dimensions. Repeat for your own image and adjust by resizing (*Image > Resize* or *Shift + S*) to match the two photographs.

HEADS UP

If you're having difficulty matching a full-length picture of yourself against that of the celebrity, try replacing just the face of the companion. With a bit of ingenuity, resizing, cloning work, and some feathering, it's quite easy to blend your face into someone else's.

3 Ask a friend to take your picture against a neutral background and posed as closely as you can manage to the companion you're going to replace in the original picture. Don't worry too much about relative sizes at this point. Reducing the new shot to match the original won't lose a great deal in quality.

5 Select your picture and draw around yourself with the *Lasso* tool (try to do this accurately so you pick as little background as possible). Pull down the *Selections* menu and choose *Feather* from the *Modify* submenu (or press *Control + H*). When the *Feather* dialogue appears, enter a value of about five pixels. You might need to experiment - the idea is to soften the edges just enough to blend them into the new picture. Press *Shift + Control + I* to select the background and delete it. Right-click to deselect. Press *Control + C* to make a copy of this image.

6 Activate the celebrity image by clicking it. Use the *Clone* tool to remove the greater part of the companion - you can do this quite roughly because your image will overlay the one you're removing. Pull down the *Edit* menu and select *Paste* (or press *Control + V*) to paste the clipboard selection into the celebrity picture.

7 Position the layer of you as closely as you can to the original. You can use the *Clone* tool to aid blending.

144-147_NewStep9a_X_DPCC_sg.tif @ 100% (RGB/8)   _ □ ✕

100%   Doc: 835.2K/835.2K

BLACK-AND-WHITE BLEND

If you're having trouble blending two colour images convincingly, try rendering both as greyscale. The eye can be more easily fooled by the subtle shades of grey.

8 To create an illusion of depth in the picture, you can create more layers by selecting bits of the original picture using the *Freehand* tool, copying them to the clipboard, and pasting them back into the picture as a new layer (*Control + L* again). In this way you can build multilayered pictures that truly blend your image with the original.

9 When the picture appears just as you want it, flatten the layers by selecting *Merge All* from the *Merge* submenu on the *Layers* menu. Finally, *Save As* by pressing *Shift + Control + S*.

LESSON 14 – DELETING RED-EYE

Let's continue the masterclass with a relatively simple, yet nevertheless highly useful technique for ridding blighted pictures of the dreaded red-eye phenomenon! This infuriatingly common occurrence is the ruin of thousands of pictures.

Red-eye is caused by light from the camera's flash illuminating, and being reflected by, the subject's retina. It happens because in dim light the pupils open wide to allow more light to enter the eye. The intense flash of light from the flashgun occurs far quicker than the eye can respond, and so it is caught by the camera while wide open, reflecting the light as a red disc.

Red-eye looks particularly unpleasant when it occurs in the eyes of pets such as dogs and cats, and though we've come to live with the phenomenon, it spoils many otherwise excellent photographs. Over the years photographers have developed techniques to try to avoid red-eye. With conventional film you only know red-eye has blighted your pictures when you get them back from the laboratory. Digital photographers can review pictures as they're taken and reshoot as necessary, but the potential for red-eye is just as strong a possibility.

Flash Compensation

Many cameras offer a red-eye-beating flash option which fires a pre-exposure flash burst, pauses momentarily while the eye adjusts itself to the new light level, and then fires the flash again. If your camera features red-eye compensation then use it. If you forget, don't have time to set it up, or didn't realise there was a potential for red-eye until you saw the spoiled pictures downloaded to your computer, here's what to do to restore them to good health...

2 Elements' *Auto Red-eye Fix* can be found under the *Enhance* menu or you can press *Control + R* on the keyboard. Elements will then automatically detect what it thinks is red-eye in your image and try to correct it. However, often the results are crude, with a flat, unnatural black replacing the equally unattractive red-eye.

Red Shift

1 Photoshop Elements, Paint Shop Pro and many other image-editing programs provide dedicated and sophisticated tools that enable you to remove red-eye in your pictures quickly and easily. Here we are using Photoshop Elements, which has an automatic red-eye fix option as well as a dedicated red-eye removal tool.

Pupil Size: 50% ▶ Darken Amount: 50% ▶ (Auto)

3 Selecting the *Red-eye Removal* tool from the toolbar gives greater control, with three settings in the options bar – *Pupil Size*, *Darken Amount* and *Auto*. The *Auto* option is again best avoided though, so just concentrate on the size/amount sliders.

4 As a rule, a large pupil size and a small darken amount is the best combination to start with, but experiment with the settings as the result will change depending on the intensity of the red-eye in your image and the size of the affected pupils.

5 To remove red-eye, first zoom into your image so you can see the pupils clearly. Using the *Red-eye Removal* tool click on the red pupil and Elements will replace the colour with a neutral grey tone.

6 If the effect of the red-eye removal is too weak then you can either press *Control + Z* to 'undo' the adjustment before increasing the darken amount and trying again, or you can click on the pupil again, using the same 'weak' setting to make a second – darker – adjustment. For this image, two clicks with the *Red-eye Removal* tool gave the desired result.

PRO OPTIONS

Paint Shop Pro provides a comprehensive red-eye removal system, with a semi-automated red-eye removal tool and a red-eye dialogue box that has comprehensive settings for both human and animal eyes.

Paint Shop Pro's red-eye tool works in a similar way to Elements' – you set the size of the tool in the options bar and click on the offending area. However, there's no control over the intensity and, like Elements' 'auto' option, the results can sometimes look unnatural.

A far more sophisticated removal system can be called up by choosing *Adjust > Red-Eye Removal* from the menu bar. Here you will find presets for human and animal eyes, as well as options that allow you to manually adjust the effect. You can even choose the eye colour and adjust the glint for a natural-looking result. Experiment with the various settings, using the preview window as a guide.

LESSON 15 – SIMPLE ANIMATION

Watch the natural world unfold at a rate of knots! Compress time using a special photographic technique known as 'time-lapse' and a hidden world around you will spring up before your lens.

Time-lapse is a variation on the theme of movie-making that uses still digital images (explored on the next pages). But unlike creating an animated film using props and stills, time-lapse photography compresses the passage of time into a very short sequence that enables you to see incredible beauty in the natural world which is otherwise missed.

Nature Blossoms

Leaves unfolding, flowers opening, the natural movement of trees, cloud formations moving overhead, seeds sprouting and growing, animated shadows as the sun moves across the sky, the hands of clocks whizzing around - you've probably seen examples of all these 'effects' elsewhere, and now you can recreate them and dream up new examples of your own. How is time compressed in this way? The camera remains still and is set to take a picture at fixed intervals over a period of time: an hour, a day, a week, or whatever. When that sequence of pictures is run together as an animation, the hidden 'movement' of the subject - which otherwise occurs so slowly that it cannot be detected - is revealed.

Many digital cameras offer an on-board time-lapse function which you can set to take time-lapse pictures automatically, thereby simplifying the process enormously. You need only set up the shot and take the first picture, and your camera does the rest. However, even cameras that do not offer time-lapse can be used to produce the effect.

Timed to Perfection

1 If your camera provides a time-lapse function, the process is easy. If it doesn't, you can still take great time-lapse sequences, but the onus will be on you to switch on the camera, take the picture, and switch it off again at whatever interval you deem suitable.

2 Set your camera on a tripod before your subject. Switch on the camera's time-lapse mode and select a suitable interval between exposures. This should be long enough to best capture the passing of time as it applies to the subject. If your camera doesn't have time-lapse, it'll be up to you to come and take the picture at the required interval.

3 Press the shutter to take the first picture, then leave the camera to do its work (returning when necessary to fire the shutter if there's no time-lapse function).

4 When the sequence is complete, download each frame to your computer and use animation software (or the *Flipbook* option in Photoshop Elements 5) to join them together in an animated sequence - you'll be amazed at the results!

Elements Flipbook

2 Next, choose *Create > Flipbook* from the menu bar. If it isn't already open, Elements will activate the image organiser (which isn't needed here) and then the *Flipbook* dialogue window.

1 To start making your Flipbook, drag the images you want to use into the Photoshop Elements photo bin at the bottom of the screen. Note that they need to be JPEG files.

3 In the *Flipbook* dialogue window you can set the parameters for your animation. You can set the speed it's played at (in frames per second), choose to reverse - or loop - the playback, and there's the option to choose the size for your final show (640x480 pixels is ideal for a computer monitor). You can preview your Flipbook in the left-hand preview window and when you're happy with it press *Output*, choose a file name in the next dialogue window and then *Save*.

LESSON 16 – MAKING MOVIES

Use your still digicam to produce short movies – or lengthy ones if you have the patience! With a few simple props and a little imagination you can even make movies featuring all kinds of characters!

Believe it or not, it's entirely possible to make your own films using your digital camera! Virtually every compact digital camera that you can buy today has a 'movie mode', and many will let your record movies until your memory card is full - so there's no limit to the length of the clips you can shoot. On top of this, many cameras will still let you use the camera's zoom lens as you film, and they will also record audio at the same time through a built in microphone.

A compact digital camera won't give quite the same quality as a dedicated video camera , but the gap is narrowing, so why not use your stills camera to shoot moving images to edit on your computer?

Hardware and software

Moving images understandably take up a lot more space than still photographs, so a large memory card is definitely recommended if you have aspirations of becoming the next Steven Spielberg. Look for 2GB (or larger) memory cards for your camera.

You will also need space on your computer for all your movie files, so consider investing in a second hard disk drive - either internal or external.

Finally, if you want to edit your clips you're going to need some video editing software. The good news is almost all new computers come with the right tools, such as Windows Movie Maker which we'll be using here.

1 The first step of making your movie is to import all the clips that you want to use in the final show. Do this by selecting *Video* from the *Import* section of the *Task Bar*. In the browser window that pops up, locate the video clips you want to use (*Shift-click* to select more than one) and then press import. Your chosen clips will appear in Windows Movie Maker between the *Preview Window* and the *Task Bar*.

Makes titles and credits you can use in your movie.

2 To start putting your clips together to make your movie you need to drag them from the *Clip Palette* to the *Storyboard* at the bottom of the main window. To build up your project continue adding clips, noting that the order they appear in the *Storyboard* is the order they will play in.

4 Once you've edited all your clips together add a professional touch by choosing *Titles and Credits* from the *Task Bar*. Here you can add a title at the start of your movie, and credits at the end.

5 Finally, as well as saving your had work to your computer you can 'publish' your movie. Choose *Publish Movie* from the top menu and then decide where you want it to be saved to - creating a DVD is a great way of sharing your film.

3 You might not always want to use a clip in its entirety, and Windows Movie Maker will let you edit your movie snippets as well. To 'cut' a clip simply click on it and play it in the *Preview Window*. When you get to the part you want to remove pause the playback and click on the *Split Clip* button to the bottom right of the *Preview Window*. This will split the clip into two in the *Storyboard* and you can delete the part you don't want, or insert a new clip between the two.

LESSON 17 – PRESERVATION

Render your existing conventional prints as digital photographs and you'll be able to rescue them from flaws and defects as easily as you can with digital pictures. Making copies isn't so difficult and requires little more than the kind of apparatus that you can find about the home.

As you become accustomed to the incredible range of options available to you as a digital photographer, you may come to wish that you could manipulate existing printed photographs in the same way. Just think: all those old prints spoiled by poor lighting, red-eye, fuzzy focusing, scratches on the negatives, tears and dog-ears could be repaired and made, well, better than new! You could rescue and make copies of irreplaceable old prints of your relatives, preserve them for posterity, and make prints to share among your family.

Scan or Shoot

Of course one option would be to invest in a scanner to make scans of your archive material (see page 151), but you can easily digitise your images using a digital camera. The only extra piece of equipment you'll need is a tripod of some description. These are relatively cheap, but you'll need to check that your camera has the necessary tripod thread - very cheap cameras often don't. A piece of wood for a baseboard, a couple of Anglepoise lamps, and an hour or two to spare, and you'll be able to copy prints easily.

Posterity Prints

1 You'll need a piece of wood for a baseboard for your prints. Any old offcut of wood measuring, say, 45x45cm is fine. Paint it matt black if you can (or cover it with a sheet of black crêpe paper available for a few pence from art suppliers if you can't). This will help stop your camera from taking false meter readings.

2 Commandeer the kitchen table for an hour or two and beg, steal, or borrow a couple of Anglepoise lamps! Place the baseboard on the table and set the lamps at either side of it so that their light floods across the baseboard at a lowish angle. Don't switch on the lamps yet (otherwise the print will curl in the heat from the bulbs).

3 Lay your print face-up on the baseboard. If it begins to curl, use a couple of rulers (or similar) laid along the edges to hold it flat. Position your camera on its tripod directly over the print so that the lens is at a right angle to it and between 30cm and 45cm away.

4 Now you'll discover why an LCD preview screen and a zoom lens can be so useful! Switch on the camera and use the zoom lens to fill as much of the LCD screen as you can with the print. It's certain that you'll need to shuffle the tripod around slightly, and make various small adjustments to get everything to line up, but persevere - the results are worth it!

5 Switch on your camera's timer function. Switch on the Anglepoise lamps. Squeeze the shutter button to focus, then fire the shutter. Let go of the camera, stand back so that you're not casting a shadow across the print, and let the camera take the picture.

Masterclass Tips

6 Review and repeat as necessary using any features your camera has, such as EV compensation, white balance, and macro focus to make the best possible copy. Don't discard any of the exposures you make until you've reviewed them all on your computer screen. It may be possible to make a better picture from a poor but digitally edited image.

7 Save, then use the tools and filters described elsewhere in this book to clean up and repair the print as necessary. *Save As*, and then commit the image to paper - you'll be amazed at the results!

SCANNERS AND SCANNING

If you have a lot of prints that you'd like to rescue, then invest in a flatbed scanner. This is a device that makes high-resolution copies of photographs, transparencies - in fact, anything you place on its glass scanning window. Resolution is typically 4800dpi and prices have never been cheaper. Advances in technology and manufacturing mean that you can get a scanner for home use for around £50, though a model that also allows you to scan film will increase the price. Most image-editing packages support scanners directly so you can acquire the image directly from your scanner.

Scanner plate

Scanning mechanism and imaging system

Focusing and collimating lens

CCD array

Flatbed scanner with
transparency hood

Flatbed scanner

Film scanner

Proving
the Pudding

Until it's printed, a digital photograph is no more than a collection of bits and bytes. True, you can create spectacular slideshows of your images on a computer, mail pictures to websites and newsgroups, and email them to your friends, but the proof of the pudding, the reality of a picture for most people, is when it's printed and displayed in a way that everyone can enjoy - even those without computers. Fortunately, high-quality printers have never been cheaper and the technology is relatively easy to use. As always though, an insight or two will enable you to really get the most from what the printer has to offer the digital camera owner.

PRINTS AND PAPER

Printing is when your previously digital images stored as bits of data on a computer become – in the eyes of most people at least – real photographs, something tangible that you can share among friends or flick through in the pages of an album…

Until now, your digital photographs have been just that: digital. No matter how well you've taken, edited, stored, or manipulated them, the pictures have only existed virtually, and been as real as a computer-generated representation can be. One tiny electrical glitch between camera and computer, and those precious bits of data could disappear forever. Of course, such glitches are rare, and once your images are held on a storage card, they're at least as safe as a package of prints. But maybe now is the time to return to the 'real world', and actually reproduce your pictures as a series of prints.

No Place like Home

There's never been a better time to explore printing at home. The technology has advanced in leaps and bounds, and today you can buy a colour printer that offers truly amazing resolution and depth of colour at well under £50. Use the device with purpose-made glossy photographic paper, and you'll create images with a quality that rivals many commercial processing outlets.

Possibly the most obvious way to display your digital photographs is to gather them together in an album of some kind. Choose one without plastic curtains, however, otherwise pictures generated on inkjet printers will soon discolour, and may even fade completely!

Digital editing and printing techniques can help you produce a stunning physical album of montages, effects, and textures that will lift your pictures off the page.

Many Happy Digital Returns

Another good print option is to select a favourite picture and turn it into a greetings card. Many laser printers and most inkjets will print quite happily on relatively heavyweight paper or greetings card paper made especially for the purpose. If yours won't print on heavier media, try printing on normal-weight paper and include trim marks; glue to pre-prepared cardboard blanks and trim to finish. And if you tailor the picture to a particular event such as Valentine's or Mother's Day, so much the better!

Been There, Got the T-shirt

Broadcast your images to the world by printing one on a T-shirt. Iron-on transfer paper is available from most inkjet paper suppliers, or you can get it done at most high-street labs. Add interest by making a montage of several pictures, insert a humorous caption, or manipulate an image to create a truly spectacular effect.

MAKING CONTACT

Conventional camera buffs, those with a home darkroom, often make 'contact' prints - direct prints from the negative without enlarging - which enable the photographer to get some idea of what the completed print will look like, but without wasting lots of expensive photographic paper in the process. By comparison, digital photographers have it easy. You can view your images on-screen, selecting only those that meet your approval for editing and ultimately printing. However, a digital 'contact' print, a single A4 sheet filled with the pictures from a particular set (and we'll discuss filing systems later in this chapter) serves a real purpose in enabling you to sift through photographs and easily select, say, the particular CD-ROM on which they're stored. It also makes for a pleasant hour or two spent poring over your hard-earned pictures!

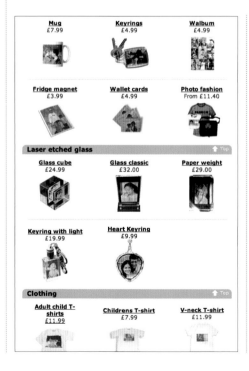

The unique advantage of digital images is that they can be output onto as many media as exist, simply by handing the file over to a specialist supplier, or mailing it to a specialist website. Mugs, bed linen, mousemats, posters, stationery... you name it, it's possible.

HARD AND FAST

Time was when the humble dot matrix and office daisywheel were the only way to get computers to print something. Now an enormous range of high-quality inkjets and some spectacular dye-subs provide near professional-quality output at home.

Printers, much like digital cameras (and perhaps even because of them!), have come a long way in the past five years or so. From being large-footprint, low-resolution devices that offered little in the way of colour, printer technology has advanced to the point where it's feasible to print photo-realistic pictures at home with very little fuss. What's more, you can buy printers that combine the functions of a scanner and a fax machine too, so that as well as being able to print digital images from your computer, you can scan traditional photographs and edit and combine them with pictures from your digital camera. The digital darkroom has truly come of age - and at an affordable price.

A Non-PC Solution

For those without a computer and who don't want to own one, many manufacturers offer printers that accept storage cards direct from the camera - eject the card from the camera, pop it into the printer, and use the printer's functions to select from a range of printing, resizing, and cropping options for true versatility, albeit without true editing options.

Resolution is as much an issue for printers as it is for cameras, although printer resolution is generally measured in dots per inch (dpi) rather than pixels per inch. Even entry-level inkjet printers typically have a resolution of 4800dpi - which is regarded as photo-quality, especially when the printer is used with photo-quality glossy paper.

Desktop inkjet printers are a low-cost means to a high-quality end, but you'll quickly use up the colour cartridges if you print out a lot of images or copies. Good-quality paper makes for professional results.

Inkjets

Inkjets (sometimes known as 'Bubblejets') are the workhorses of the photo printing world. They're easy to use and set up, and ink cartridges are widely available, and occasionally refillable! Resolution is in the order of 4800dpi, even for a sub-£100 printer, which is more than adequate for quality home printing, especially if you use photo-quality glossy paper.

An inkjet requires only a small amount of space on your desktop, produces little noise and no fumes, so it's ideal where space is at a

premium, such as when sharing a computer system with the rest of the family, or if you have a home office. A reasonable quality entry-level colour inkjet printer can cost as little as £50, while £200 will get you a fast, high-resolution inkjet capable of near-commercial results. For a little bit more you can buy an A3 printer for even larger prints.

Dye-subs

Dye-sublimation printers ('dye-subs') transfer colour ink from a ribbon onto a special paper using heat. Quality can be high, and unlike inkjet printers each ink ribbon produces a set number of prints - so you know exactly how much each print will cost. Dye-sub printers are slow though, because the paper has to pass through the printer four times and they don't reproduce type well. The output is small compared with other types - often only A6 (100x148mm) - but the future promises much for the technology and they're great if all you want are 6x4inch prints to put in an album.

Multifunctionals

Combining an inkjet printer and scanner in one unit, multifunctionals or 'all-in-ones' are an appealing option to many digital photography enthusiasts. They take up far less space than having an individual scanner and printer, often cost less and also let you make 'photocopies'. Some even work as fax machines too. Many new models have print and scan resolutions that match high-quality enthusiast printers/scanners, as well as memory card slots so you can print directly from your camera's memory card.

(Left) The image shows just how far inkjet printers have come in the last two to three years. Colours are vibrant and resolution on most models is excellent. It is only really close up that the image starts to degrade.

PAPERWEIGHTS

People quality – finish, weight, chemical additives, and fibre density – can have a profound effect on the way your digital images reproduce as prints, and on their lifespan too. Don't turn that page!

Your choice of paper is as important - arguably more so - than your choice of printer. Even a humble inkjet will produce good prints of your digital images (as long as they're of reasonable resolution in the first place), but choose the 'wrong' paper and you're guaranteed to be disappointed with the results. However, the increasing popularity of digital photography has brought with it an awareness of photographers' requirements, and photo-quality printing papers and inks, ultra-fast printers, ultraviolet-shielded picture frames, and other goodies are now available to assist you.

It is certainly possible to print photographs at home that rival the quality of commercial processing and printing, and a little experimenting with papers and inks, together with a certain amount of care with the finished prints, will produce good results.

Photo Ink

And it isn't just the paper that will affect your print quality - ink too has a part to play. Most manufacturers offer specially formulated printing inks, with an increasingly wide range of colours for photo-realistic reproduction. Having more inks can start to get expensive though, so look for a printer where you can change individual colour cartridges.

Paperstocks Explained

Budget-priced copier paper

High-street stationary suppliers often have reams of copier paper at very low prices. Although these are fine for pages of text, the coarse fibres in the paper tend to diffuse ink, creating a 'spidery' edge effect that reduces the effective resolution. Use a lot of this cheap paper and you may also find that the delicate mechanisms within your printer become clogged with paper dust (fibers that have broken free). It's best used for thumbnails rather than your prized photographs.

Ordinary printer/copier paper

Good-quality printer and copier paper has more densely packed, finer fibres that inhibit ink diffusion, and create slightly better prints. However, you'll pay more than twice as much for a ream as for budget copier paper, and the results from digital images still won't be anywhere near as good as those from photo papers. Colour reproduction and contrast will appear dull, flat, and lifeless (by comparison), though it won't clog your printer as readily as the cheap stuff! Good for test prints, thumbnails/image catalogue prints and letters, but still not ideal for photographs.

Coated paper/inkjet paper

Coated inkjet paper is intended for colour image outputting. It contains special coatings that inhibit ink diffusion and smudging and help make inks 'fast' (fixed) so prints last for many years without fading. The quality of digital images printed on coated paper is significantly improved over 'ordinary' photocopy style paper types, making it great for everyday prints. More and more paper manufacturers now provide textured 'art' papers as well.

Glossy photo paper

As you might expect, glossy photo paper is the best of all for printing digital photographs. Intensely white and with a coating that lends a vibrancy to coloured printer inks, glossy photo paper is as close as you'll get to commercially printed photographs. It's more expensive than the other types, especially when you choose a 'heavyweight' gloss paper, but the results will almost certainly be worth it. Use it to make enlargements of your favorite prints - those you want to frame, perhaps?

Tiger, tiger, burning bright... but not in the forests of poor-quality paper. The image *(left)* shows just how well a good-quality photo paper can bring your images to life, and make them as crisp as they appeared on your computer monitor.

HIGH STREET CONFIDENTIAL

If you don't yet own a printer but want the convenience of paper-based pictures, take advantage of the increasing number of high-street and online processing outlets that offer a variety of digital output services.

There's one very real 'danger' when using a digital camera: that many of your photographs will remain only as bits of data on a computer. In one sense that's a bonus because you have the opportunity to review and edit each image before committing it to print. However, once the initial excitement of instant digital photography has worn off it's sometimes an effort to muster the energy even to bother to switch on your computer, let alone spool through hundreds of images, selecting, editing, and printing them. At times like that, the thought of simply collecting a package of pictures from a high-street photographic processing service and flicking through them in the comfort of your favourite armchair can be an attractive one indeed!

Bureaux of Change

Even if some of the pictures are a disappointment - if only you'd cropped that image, or painted in a different sky! - the ease with which you can enjoy them without the buzz of a computer and the whir a of a printer is a weighty counterbalance to inconvenience. And that's not all. Few are the friends who want to stand beside your computer to see your pictures - they'd far rather be handed a sheaf of photographs to flick through.

What many digital photographers don't realise is that high-street processing is entirely possible even if you're using the very latest in digital marvels. Many traditional processing labs will cheerfully accept your digital memory cards and hand you back a package of glossy prints, just as if you'd given them a conventional film for processing!

Commercial Breakdown

Before you try, there are several things to bear in mind - the first and most important is don't hand over your card direct from your camera - unless you're absolutely sure that what's stored there is fit for reproduction!

There are plenty of online services on the internet that will print your digital photographs onto photographic paper, and you can also buy other gifts, including 'photo books'. Simply post your digital images onto the site, select the layout style and type of album you want and, within a few days, you will receive a professional looking album of your chosen photos.

ONLINE OUTPUT

In the spirit of all things digital, many Web-based processing services can accept emailed images and will send prints by return in the mail. This is an option that's definitely worth considering if you have high-speed Internet access. Here's how to get your prints ready to 'upload'.

1 Download your pictures to your computer, and select those fit for printing. Edit the selected images so that you can be sure they'll be reproduced at their best. Jobs to do might be to balance contrast, brighten colours and tweak backgrounds and compositions.

2 It's useful to resize your images next, so that when you upload them to an online lab the files are optimised for the size of prints you want, and also small enough to send over the Internet quickly.

3 Using the *Image Size* tool in Photoshop Elements, set your picture so that it's the same dimensions (or as close as possible) to the intended print size and the resolution is between 200dpi and 300dpi. This will give the best 'photographic' print quality.

4 Now that your picture is at the right size, it's time to save it in the right format. Because you'll be sending your pictures to the lab using the Internet they need to be compressed, so they should always be saved as JPEG files.

5 Choose *File > Save As*, enter a suitable name for the new image, and save it as a JPEG file. Repeat steps 3-5 for all the images in your selection and you're ready to start uploading them to your chosen lab.

iPhoto offers an amazing variety of options once you have loaded your images into the software. You can arrange your photos for albums, view them in a slide show, and undertake minor editing tasks.

iPhoto also features software that enables you to set up a slide show. You can choose how long each image is displayed, its size, and even appropriate music, before exporting it as a QuickTime movie.

RANK AND FILE

Digital photography positively encourages you to get out there and take lots of pictures! Not for digital photographers the worry of wasting expensive film, nor the concerns over processing costs for pictures which might never see the light of day.

With a digital camera you can take endless pictures and store thousands of them on even a modest modern PC or Mac with little fear of running out of space. But the only way you'll find an image is by establishing a filing system and sticking to it. Fortunately for owners of new PCs, Windows Vista is a great aid in that it provides all kinds of tracking tools to enable you to store, browse, and watch slideshows of your pictures. Similarly, Mac OS X provides similar facilities in its iLife software options.

If you want to create a more permanent store, a CD (or DVD) recorder is a must. Arguably the perfect storage medium, CD and DVDs are thought to have a shelf life of around 100 years, so it'll be a while before you have to consider updating and refreshing your picture archive!

CD Burning – PC

Burning a CD or DVD used to require special software that was often more complicated than it needed to be, but with the Windows Vista operating system burning a folder of images is a much simpler 'one click' operation.

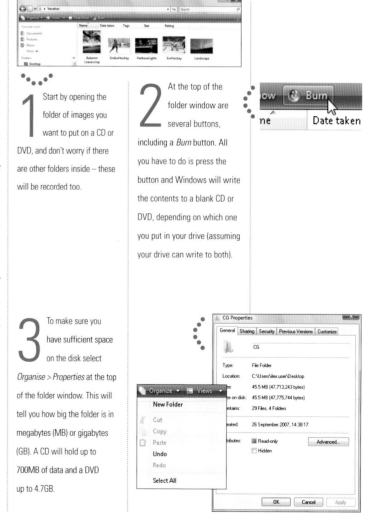

1 Start by opening the folder of images you want to put on a CD or DVD, and don't worry if there are other folders inside – these will be recorded too.

2 At the top of the folder window are several buttons, including a *Burn* button. All you have to do is press the button and Windows will write the contents to a blank CD or DVD, depending on which one you put in your drive (assuming your drive can write to both).

3 To make sure you have sufficient space on the disk select *Organise > Properties* at the top of the folder window. This will tell you how big the folder is in megabytes (MB) or gigabytes (GB). A CD will hold up to 700MB of data and a DVD up to 4.7GB.

CD Burning – Mac

As with the latest version of Windows, burning a CD or DVD on a modern Apple Mac is incredibly straightforward, and doesn't require any additional software. However, the process is a little different.

1 Begin by checking how large your folder of images is. To do this, locate your image folder and select *File > Info* from the Finder menu. A window will open telling you how much space the folder takes up – up to 700MB will fit on a CD and up to 4.7GB will require a DVD.

3 In the bar running down the side of your finder windows you will now have a CD icon called *Untitled* with a burn icon next to it. Click on the icon and drag the files and folders you want to burn onto the disc into the window – just as you would normally to move or copy files from one window to another. Note that the files aren't copied or moved, they are just referenced.

4 When you have all your files in the *Untitled CD* window click *Burn* at the top right. A dialogue will ask if you're sure and you can enter a new title for the disk. Choose the *Burn Speed* from the drop down menu (fast for speed, or slower for reliability) and click the blue *Burn* button. Your Mac will now record the files onto your CD or DVD.

2 Insert your blank CD or DVD into your CD/DVD burner and a dialogue window will appear on screen, asking you what you want to do. Choose *Open Finder*, and if you want this to happen automatically in the future check the *Make this action the default* box before pressing *OK*.

DVD slideshows

There are plenty of programs available that will let you create a slideshow, some of which you can buy, some that come as part of an image-editing program, and others that can be downloaded freely from the internet. However, if you've recently bought a new PC you'll probably find Windows Movie Maker, which is part of Windows Vista. This is a great way of creating slideshows of your pictures to share with friends and family.

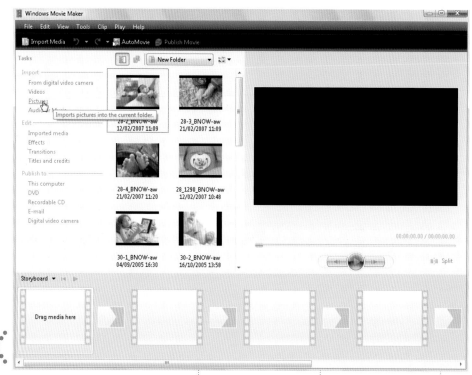

1 To start making a slideshow you need to import some pictures. Click the *Pictures* button under the *Import* options on the left hand *Task Bar* and choose your images from the file browser window. Remember, you can *Shift-click* to select a range of images or *Control-click* to select multiple images one at a time. When you've chosen the pictures you want in your show, press the *Import* button and watch as your selected images appear between the *Task Bar* and the *Preview Window*.

2 The next step is to set how long you want your slides to appear on screen (4-5 seconds is normally long enough). Select *Tools > Options* from the tool bar, and the *Advanced* tab from the dialogue that pops up. Enter the time in the *Picture Duration* field and the time you would like any transitions to play for (fades/dissolves etc.) in the *Transition Duration* (around one second is good).

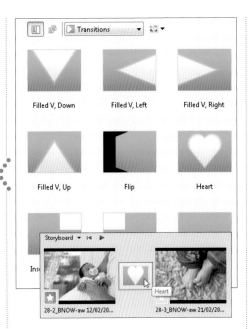

3 To start putting your images into a slideshow drag the image thumbnails into the *Storyboard* frames at the bottom of the Movie Maker window. You can *Shift-click* to select a range of images and drag them as a batch, and the order they appear in the *Storyboard* if the order they will be played in.

4 You can add special effects to your storyboarded images by opening the effect options (click *Effects* on the *Task Bar*) and dragging/dropping your chosen effect onto the small star icon at the bottom left of the image previews on the storyboard.

5 You can also add transitions, so your images fade in and out, dissolve into one another or wipe across the screen, among numerous other effects. Click *Transitions* in the *Task Bar* to open the *Transitions Palette*. Drag the transition you want to use onto the storyboard, dropping it into the box between the images you want it to affect.

6 You can use the *Preview Window* to see how your slideshow will look and when all your images, effects and transitions are how you want them you are ready to 'publish' the project. There are a number of *Publish To* options under the *Task Bar*, including options to record your slideshow to your computer's hard disc, a CD or DVD, as an email attachment, or even record it onto a digital video camera.

Publish to
This computer
DVD
Recordable CD
E-mail
Digital video camera

POST HASTE

Once upon a time if you wanted to mail photographs to your friends and relatives you had to find a padded envelope or corrugated stiffener inserts, pay the extortionate postage seemingly required for anything heavier than the envelope, and wait the week or so until they were delivered. Nowadays, there's email...

Unlike paper-based communications, email is more or less instant; write your email, address it, and click the Send button. A fraction of a second later the recipient can be reading it, wherever they are, as long as they have access to a computer - with wireless internet access they don't even need a phone line! And what's good for simple text messages can also be used for sending pictures - though a certain amount of 'cheating' is required.

Encoded Only

Designed as a text-only medium, the underlying email technology has to be fooled into believing that what is being sent consists only of plain text. Send a picture with an email as an 'attachment' and it must undergo a process known as 'UUencoding'. This means that the data that describes the digital picture is made to look like plain text to the email server. As you might imagine, an 'encoded' email must be 'decoded' at the receiving end. Once, the encode/decode process was manual - you had to feed your attachments to a separate utility program. Now the email client (the software you use to send emails) does the encoding and decoding for you, on the fly.

Steps to Send

1 To send a digital photograph as an attachment, first use your image-editing software to reduce its size by resizing and/or resampling the picture.

2 A compression program such as WinZip (PC) or StuffIt (Mac) can be used to reduce file sizes, but usually, saving a copy of the image as a JPEG file will make it small enough to send by email.

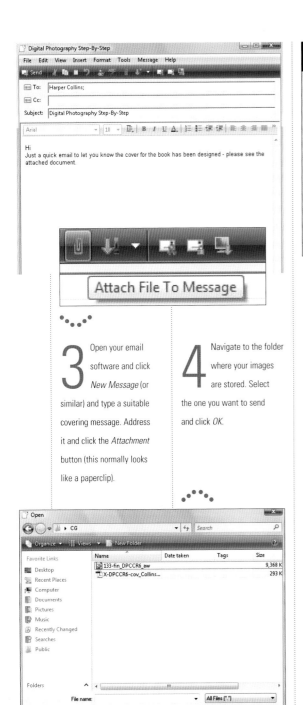

WORDS TO THE WISE

While it's perfectly possible to send digital images as email attachments, it isn't always sensible. A digital photograph can be several megabytes in size and if you attach an album's worth the recipient could be downloading for days! What's more, some companies place a restriction on the size of mailboxes - send an email with many large attachments and you might find it's simply bounced back to you. The best practise is to send image files no larger than 2MB (megabytes) and to send images this size one at a time.

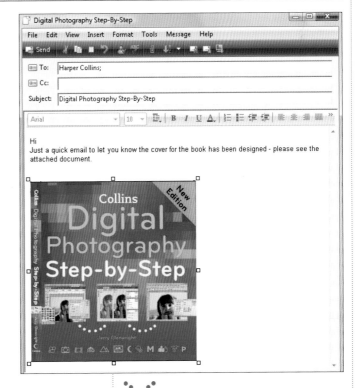

3 Open your email software and click *New Message* (or similar) and type a suitable covering message. Address it and click the *Attachment* button (this normally looks like a paperclip).

4 Navigate to the folder where your images are stored. Select the one you want to send and click *OK*.

5 Click *Send* and your email software will connect to your ISP and begin to upload (transfer) your email and its attachments to the mail server. The time this will take depends on the total size of your attachments.

GLOSSARY

A

Adobe US company that develops software for specialist, creative tasks such as Web design, graphic design, and video editing. Its products are widely used by both professionals and amateurs. Photoshop, Photoshop Elements, and Lightroom are its most successful image-editing software products.

alpha channel A greyscale version of an image that can be used in conjunction with the other three colour channels, such as for creating a mask.

animation The process of creating a moving image by rapidly moving from one still image to the next. Animations are now commonly created by specialist software that renders sequences in a variety of formats.

anti-aliasing The smoothing of jagged edges on diagonal lines created in an imaging program, by giving intermediate values to pixels between the steps.

application Software designed to make the computer perform a specific task. So, image-editing is an application, as is word-processing. System software, however, is not an application, as it controls the running of the computer.

artefact Any flaw in a digital image, such as 'noise'. Most artefacts are undesirable, although adding 'noise' can create a desirable grainy texture if the image is appropriate.

B

back-up A copy of either a file or a program created in case the original becomes damaged (corrupt) or lost.

bit depth The number of bits-per-pixel (usually per channel, sometimes for all the channels combined), which determines the number of colours it can display. Eight bits-per-

channel are needed for photo-quality imaging.

bitmap graphic An image made up of dots, or pixels, and usually produced by painting or image-editing applications (as distinct from the vector images of 'object-orientated' drawing applications). The more pixels used for one image, the higher its resolution. This is the normal form of a digital photograph.

browser/Web browser Program that enables the viewing or 'browsing' of World Wide Web pages across the Internet. The most commonly used browsers are Microsoft's Internet Explorer, Mozilla Firefox and Safari. Version numbers are important, as these indicate the level of HTML that the browser supports, its performance, and the level of security it offers.

burn(ing) The act of recording data onto a CD or DVD in a CD/DVD burner (recorder). Software such as Roxio's Toast (Mac) is used for this task when recording

from a computer to an external recorder.

byte Eight bits - the basic data unit of computing.

C

CD-ROM CD (Compact Disc) Read-Only Memory. An evolution of the CD allowing the storage of up to 600 megabytes of data, such as images, video clips, text, and other digital files. But the discs are 'read only', which means the user can't edit or overwrite the data.

CD-R/CD-RW CD CD-Recordable/ CD-ReWriteable. CD-Rs are inexpensive discs on which you can store any digital data, or roughly 77 minutes of audio. Once written and finalised (fixed), the data cannot be erased, edited, or modified. CD-RW disks can be 'unfinalised' and overwritten, in part or entirely, any number of times.

channel Part of an image as stored in the computer; similar to a layer. Commonly, a colour image will have a channel allocated to each primary or process colour, and sometimes one or more for a mask or other effect.

clone/cloning In most image-editing packages, Clone tools allow the user to sample pixels from one part of an image, such as a digital photograph, and use them to 'paint' over other areas of the image. The process is useful for removing unwanted parts of an image, or correcting problems, such as closed eyes if the subject blinked while being photographed. In Photoshop and Photoshop Elements, the tool is also known as the Rubber Stamp.

colour depth See BIT DEPTH

colour gamut The range of colour that can be produced by an output device, such as a printer, a monitor, or a film recorder.

colour picker The term describing a colour model when displayed on a computer monitor. Colour pickers may be specific to an application such as

Adobe Photoshop, a third-party colour model such as PANTONE, or to the operating system running on your computer.

compression The technique of rearranging data so that it either occupies less space on disc, or transfers faster between devices or over communication lines. For example, high-quality digital images, such as photographs, can take up an enormous amount of disk space, transfer slowly, and use a lot of processing power. They need to be compressed (the file size needs to be made smaller) before they can be published on the Web, as otherwise they would take too long to appear onscreen. But compressing them can lead to a loss of quality. Compression methods that do not lose data are referred to as 'lossless', while 'lossy' describes methods in which some data is lost.

continuous-tone image An image, such as a photograph, in which there is a smooth progression of tones between black and white.

contrast The degree of difference between adjacent tones in an image from the lightest to the darkest. 'High contrast' describes an image with light highlights and dark shadows, but with few shades in between, while a 'low contrast' image is one with even tones and few dark areas or highlights. These settings are usually editable.

copyright The right of a person who creates an original work to protect that work by controlling how and where it may be reproduced.

copyright-free A misnomer used to describe ready-made resources, such as clip-art. In fact, these resources are rarely, if ever, 'copyright free'. Generally it is only the licence to use the material which is granted by purchase. 'Royalty free' is a more accurate description.

D

digitise To convert anything, for example, text, images, or sound, into binary form so that it can be digitally processed. In other words,

transforming analogue data into digital data.

dithering The technique of appearing to show more colours than are actually being used, by mingling pixels. A complex pattern of intermingling adjacent pixels of two colours gives the illusion of a third colour, although this gives a much lower resolution.

dots per inch (dpi) A unit of measurement used to represent the resolution of devices such as printers and also, erroneously, monitors and images, whose resolution should more properly be expressed in pixels per inch (ppi). The closer the dots or pixels (the more there are to each inch) the better the quality. Typical resolutions are 72 ppi for a monitor, 600 dpi for a laser printer, and 1200 dpi (or more) for an inkjet printer.

download To transfer data from a remote computer, such as an Internet server, to your own. The opposite of upload.

DVD Digital Video (or Versatile) Disc. Similar in appearance to CDs, DVDs have a storage capacity of up to 4.7 gigabytes (far higher than CDs) and can deliver data at a higher rate. DVD drives (players) are now standard on many new PCs, and most will also operate as DVD writers so you can 'burn' your own DVD discs.

E

EPS (Encapsulated PostScript) Image file format for object-oriented graphics, as in drawing programs and page-layout programs.

extract A tool and a process in many image-editing applications, such as Photoshop Elements, which allows the selection of part of an image (using the selection tools) and the removal of areas around it.

Eyedropper tool In some applications, a tool for gauging the colour of adjacent pixels.

F

file extension The term describing the abbreviated suffix at the end of a filename that describes either its type (such as .eps or .jpg) or origin (the application that created it, such as .indd for InDesign files).

file format The way a program arranges data so that it can be stored or displayed on a computer. Common file formats are TIFF and JPEG for bitmapped image files, EPS for object-oriented image files, and ASCII for text files.

FireWire A type of port connection that allows for high-speed transfer of data between a computer and peripheral devices. Available in two speeds - FireWire 400 and FireWire 800.

frame A single still picture from a movie or animation sequence. Also a single image from a TV picture.

font Set of characters sharing the same typeface and size.

font file The file of a bitmapped or screen font, usually residing in a suitcase file on Mac computers.

G

GB (Gigabyte) Approximately one billion bytes (actually 1,073,741,824).

GIF (Graphics Interchange Format) One of the main bitmapped image formats used on the Internet. GIF is a 256-colour format with two specifications, GIF87a and, more recently, GIF89a, the latter providing additional features such as the use of transparent backgrounds. The GIF format uses a 'lossless' compression technique, or 'algorithm', and thus does not squeeze files as much as the JPEG format, which is 'lossy.' For use in Web browsers, JPEG is the format of choice for tone images, such as photographs, while GIF is more suitable for line images and other graphics.

graduation/gradation/ gradient The smooth transition from one colour/ tone to another. The relationship of reproduced lightness values to original lightness values in an imaging process, usually expressed as a tone curve.

H

histogram A 'map' of the distribution of tones in an image, arranged as a graph. The horizontal axis is in 256 steps from solid to empty, and the vertical axis is the number of pixels.

HSL (Hue, Saturation, Lightness) A colour model based upon the light transmitted either in an image or in your monitor - hue being the spectral colour (the actual pigment colour), saturation being the intensity of the colour pigment (without black or white added), and brightness representing the strength of luminance from light to dark (the amount of black or white present). Variously called HLS (hue, lightness, saturation), HSV (hue, saturation, value) and HSB (hue, saturation, brightness).

hue A colour found in its pure state in the spectrum.

I

icon An on-screen graphical representation of an object (such as a disc, file, folder, or tool) or a concept, used to make identification and selection easier.

interface This is a term most often used to describe the screen design that links the user with the computer program or website. The quality of the user interface often determines how well users will be able to navigate their way around the pages within the site.

interpolation Bitmapping procedure used in resizing an image to maintain resolution. When the number of pixels is increased, interpolation fills in the gaps by comparing the values of adjacent pixels.

ISP (Internet Service Provider) An organisation that provides access to the Internet. At its most basic this may be a telephone number for connection, but most ISPs provide email addresses and webspace for new sites.

J

JPEG, JPG The Joint Photographic Experts Group. An ISO (International Standards Organisation) group that defines compression standards for bitmapped colour images. The abbreviated form, pronounced 'jay-peg', gives its name to a 'lossy' (meaning some data may be lost) compressed file format in which the degree of compression from high compression and low quality, to low compression and high quality, can be defined by the user.

K

KB (Kilobyte) Approximately one thousand bytes (actually 1,024 bytes).

L

lasso A selection tool used to draw an outline around an area of the image.

layer One level of an image file, separate from the rest, allowing different elements to be edited.

lossless/lossy Refers to the data-losing qualities of different compression methods. 'Lossless' means that no image information is lost, while 'lossy' means that some (or much) of the image data is lost in the compression process (but the data will download quicker).

luminosity Brightness of colour. This does not affect the hue or colour saturation.

M

mask A greyscale template that hides part of an image. One of the most important tools in editing an image, it is used to make changes to a limited area. A mask is created by using one of the several selection tools in an image-editing program. These isolate a picture element from its surroundings, and this selection can then be moved or altered independently.

MB (Megabyte) Approximately one million bytes (actually 1,048,576).

menu An on-screen list of choices available to the user.

midtones/middletones The range of tonal values in an image anywhere between the darkest and lightest, usually referring to those approximately halfway.

multimedia Any combination of various digital media, such as sound, video, animation, graphics and text, incorporated into a software product or presentation.

N

noise Random pattern of small spots on a digital image that are generally unwanted and caused by non-image forming electrical signals. Noise is a type of artefact.

P

pixel (picture element) The smallest component of any digitally generated image, including text, such as a single dot of light on a computer screen. In its simplest form, one pixel corresponds to a single bit: 0 = off (or white) and 1 = on (or black). In colour or greyscale images one pixel may correspond to several bits. An 8-bit pixel, for example, can be displayed in any of 256 colours (the total number of different configurations that can be achieved by eight 0s and 1s).

pixels per inch (ppi) A measure of resolution for a bitmapped image.

plug-in Subsidiary software for a browser or other package that enables it to perform additional functions, e.g., play sound, movies, or video.

PNG (Portable Network Graphics) A file format for images used on the Web, which provides 10–30% 'lossless' compression. It was created as an alternative to the GIF file format.

R

RAM (Random Access Memory) The working memory of a computer, to which the central processing unit (CPU) has direct, immediate access.

raster(isation) Deriving from the Latin word *'rastrum'*, meaning rake. The method of displaying (and creating) images employed by video screens, and thus computer monitors, in which the screen image is made up of a pattern of several hundred parallel lines created by an electron beam 'raking' the screen from top to bottom at a speed of about one–sixtieth of a second. An image is created by varying the intensity of the beam at successive points along the raster. The speed at which a complete screen image, or frame, is created is called the 'frame' or 'refresh' rate.

rasterise(d) To rasterise is to electronically convert a vector graphics image into a bitmapped image. This may introduce aliasing, but is often necessary when preparing images for the Web; without a plug-in, browsers can only display bitmap image files.

resolution (1) The degree of quality, definition, or clarity with which an image is reproduced or displayed in a photograph, or via a scanner, monitor, printer, or other output device.

resolution (2) Monitor/ screen resolution. The number of pixels across by pixels down (i.e. 640 x 480, 800 x 600 and 1,024 x 768).

re-sampling Changing the resolution of an image either by removing pixels (lowering the resolution) or adding them by interpolation (increasing the resolution).

RGB (Red, Green, Blue) The primary colours of the 'additive' colour model used in video technology, computer monitors, and for graphics such as for the Web and multimedia that will not ultimately be printed by the four-colour (CMYK) process. CMYK stands for Cyan, Magenta, Yellow, and 'Key' (Black).

ROM (Read-Only Memory) Memory, such as on a CD-ROM, which can only be read, not written to. It retains its contents without power, unlike RAM.

Rubber stamp A tool in an image-editing program used to clone one selected area of the picture onto another. It allows painting with a texture rather than a single tone/colour, and is particularly useful for extending complex textures.

S

software Programs that enable a computer to perform tasks, from its operating system to job-specific applications such as image-editing programs.

T

thumbnail A small representation of an image used mainly for identification purposes in an image directory listing or, within Photoshop, for illustrating channels and layers. Thumbnails are also produced to accompany PictureCDs, PhotoCDs, and most 35-mm films submitted for processing.

TIFF (Tagged Image File Format) A standard and popular graphics file format originally developed by Aldus (now merged with Adobe) and Microsoft, used for scanned, high-resolution, bitmapped images and for colour separations. The lossless TIFF format can be used for greyscale and colour images that have been generated on different computer platforms.

tile, tiling Repeating a graphic item and placing the repetit-ions side-by-side so that they form a pattern.

toolbox A set of programs available for the computer user, each of which creates a particular on-screen effect.

transparency Allows a GIF image to be blended into the background by ridding it of unwanted background colour.

tween(ing) A contraction of 'in-between'. An animator's term for the process of creating transitional frames to fill in between key frames in an animation.

typeface The term (based on 'face' - the printing surface of a metal type character) describing a type design of any size, including weight variations on that design such as light and bold, but excluding all other related designs such as italic.

U

USB (Universal Serial Bus) An interface standard developed to replace serial and parallel ports. It allows peripherals to be plugged and unplugged while the computer is switched on - known as 'hot swapping'.

V

vector A mathematical description of a line that is defined in terms of physical dimensions and direction.

Vectors are used in drawing packages (and Photoshop 6 upwards) to define shapes (vector graphics) that are position- and size-independent.

vector graphics Images made up of mathematically defined shapes, such as circles and rectangles, or complex paths built out of mathematically defined curves. Vector graphics images can be displayed at any size or resolution without loss of quality, and are easy to edit because the shapes retain their identity, but they lack the tonal subtlety of bitmapped images.

W

webpage A published HTML document on the World Wide Web which, when linked with others, forms a website, along with other files, such as graphics.

Web server A computer ('host') that is dedicated to Web services.

website The address, location (on a server), and collection of documents and resources for any particular interlinked set of web pages.

Windows Operating system for PCs developed by Microsoft using a graphic interface that imitated that of the Macintosh.

World Wide Web (WWW) The term used to describe the entire collection of Web servers all over the world that are connected to the Internet. The term also describes the particular type of Internet access architecture that uses a combination of HTML and various graphic formats, such as GIF and JPEG, to publish formatted text that can be read by Web browsers.

INDEX

BIBLIOGRAPHY AND USEFUL ADDRESSES

BOOKS

Digital imaging and photography

Adobe Photoshop Lightroom Essentials
John Beardsworth,
Lark Books,
New York 2007

Collins Digital SLR Handbook
John Freeman,
Collins,
London 2007

The Complete Guide to Light and Lighting in Digital Photography
Michael Freeman,
Lark Books,
New York 2007

Complete Photography Manual
Steve Bavister et al,
Collins,
London 2007

Digital Photography Handbook
Tim Daly,
Argentum,
London 2000

The Photographer's Eye
Michael Freeman,
Focal Press,
London 2007

Silver Pixels
Tom Ang,
Argentum,
London 1999

WEBSITES

Note that website addresses may often change, and sites appear and disappear with alarming regularity.

Photoshop sites (tutorials, information, galleries)

Absolute Cross Tutorials
(including plug-ins)
www.absolutecross.com/
tutorials/photoshop.htm

Laurie McCanna's Photoshop Tips
www.mccannas.com/
pshop/photosh0.htm

Planet Photoshop
(portal for all things Photoshop)
www.planetphotoshop.com

Photoshop Today
www.designertoday.com/
tutorials/photoshop.aspx

Software

Photoshop, Photoshop Elements
www.adobe.com

Paintshop Pro, Photo-Paint, CorelDRAW!
www.corel.com

PhotoImpact, PhotoExpress
www.ulead.com

Toast Titanium
www.roxio.com

USEFUL ADDRESSES

Adobe (Photoshop,Illustrator)
www.adobe.com

Agfa
www.agfa.com

Alien Skin
(Photoshop Plug-ins)
www.alienskin.com

Apple Computer
www.apple.com

Canon
www.canon.co.uk

Corel
www.corel.com

Epson
www.epson.co.uk
www.epson.com

Extensis
www.extensis.com

Fujifilm
www.fujifilm.com

Hewlett-Packard
www.hp.com

Iomega
www.iomega.com

Kodak
www.kodak.com

Lexmark
www.lexmark.co.uk

Linotype
www.linotype.com

LaCie
www.lacie.com

Microsoft
www.microsoft.com

Nikon
www.nikon.com

Olympus
www.olympus.co.uk
www.olympusamerica.com

Pantone
www.pantone.com

Philips
www.philips.com

Photographic information site
www.ephotozine.com

Polaroid
www.polaroid.com

Ricoh
www.ricoh-europe.com

Samsung
www.samsung.com

Sanyo
www.sanyo.co.jp

Shutterfly
(Digital Prints via the web)
www.shutterfly.com

Sony
www.sony.com

Sun Microsystems
www.sun.com

Symantec
www.symantec.com

Umax
www.umax.com

Wacom
(graphics tablets)
www.wacom.com